At the King's Table

At the King's Table

Royal Dining Through the Ages

Susanne Groom

Foreword by
Heston Blumenthal

MERRELL
LONDON · NEW YORK

In association with
**Historic
Royal Palaces**

Foreword
Heston Blumenthal

My interest in historical British cookery actually began when I read a fifteenth-century French cookbook called *The Vivendier*. Within its pages was a recipe for preparing a chicken so it looks cooked but awakens just as it is about to be carved, and sets off down the table 'upsetting jugs, goblets and whatnot'. Until that point I had had no idea that the cookery of the past could be so dramatic and playful. I began to explore further, met two brilliant food historians called Marc Meltonville and Richard Fitch who work in the Hampton Court kitchens, and became completely absorbed by old British cookbooks and what they had to offer. In 2011 I opened a new restaurant called Dinner, with a menu that draws inspiration from nearly six centuries of British culinary history.

Much of that history is dominated by the monarchy. The oldest extant English cookbook, *The Forme of Cury*, was written around 1390 by the cooks of Richard II, and many of the landmark cookbooks of the succeeding centuries have royal connections, such as *The Queens Closet Opened* (1655), a collection of recipes and remedies from the wife of Charles I, and *Royal Cookery* (1710) by Patrick Lamb, who was master cook for four British monarchs. The sheer size of the royal household (so lavish in Richard II's time that it was claimed, undoubtedly with some exaggeration, that it employed 3000 kitchen staff) was such that a great deal of documentation, in the form of menus, account books and so on, was necessary to keep it running smoothly. It is these documents that form the backbone of the history of cooking in this country.

From such documents and other sources, Susanne Groom has drawn a fascinating portrait of royal dining through the ages. There is, as you would expect, a great sense of spectacle and extravagance among these pages. James I and Charles I were both treated to extraordinary banquets given by the Duke of Buckingham, whose most celebrated *coup de théâtre* was, apparently, the presentation of a pie out of which leapt a very small boy dressed as a knight. And the menu for a dinner given by the Prince Regent in 1817 – reproduced in all its glorious detail in the chapter 'The King of Cooks Meets the King of Gluttons' – will have you simultaneously salivating and quailing at the sheer quantity of dishes served up.

Eating is such a fundamental human activity that cooking has forever been used as a way to show off wealth and status – to demonstrate, in fact, that you're a big cheese – and this is particularly true of royalty. In 1520, at a kind of summit meeting known as the Field of Cloth of Gold, Henry VIII and François I indulged in just such one-upmanship, conducting jousts, erecting opulent tents (and spying on each other's to see if they were better) and serving up thousands of crayfish, rabbits, oxen, peacocks and porpoises at extravagant banquets. The poet John Skelton dismissed it as '... moche excesse/With banketynge braynlesse', and Groom here describes the event with a telling eye for the comic detail, such as the fact that the French king's principal tent was so tall – 120 feet – that it collapsed, disrupting the jousting. Kingly indulgence means this book is full of similarly ridiculous moments, from tables that collapse under the weight of food on them to the beguiling picture of Charles I failing to escape from Carisbrooke Castle through a window because he had eaten too well during his imprisonment and put on weight.

At the King's Table takes us from the sad plight of Richard II, deliberately starved to death in Pontefract Castle, to the modesty in 1947 of Elizabeth II's wedding breakfast, which was limited by the privations of post-war Britain, where even the royals had ration books issued in their own names. In between, it introduces us to the strange rituals of court dining, to Charles II's futile attempt to outlaw coffee houses, and to plenty more besides. It is an entertaining and insightful look at our country's history, and a great celebration of food at its most magnificent.

Introduction

'Food comes first, then morals.'

Bertolt Brecht

'Food, glorious food!' – the exclamation of the hungry and the poor; the cry that fills the moment, as that first mouthful hits the empty belly. Meanwhile the rich may buy all the food they can eat, and use it to entertain wealthy and influential acquaintances, so augmenting their standing. The monarch is in the unique and curious position of having no need to enhance his or her status and, in theory, of being able to summon whatever he or she fancies to eat, to have it prepared by renowned cooks and then wait (a moment or two) for it to be served up on silver-gilt dishes. Adventurers will scour faraway lands, the depths of the sea and the clouds of remote mountains to bring back unknown delights for the sovereign to savour. They will do it for the glory of the

ich tint le Roys de Engleterre e ilput le [...] Somer
le dieu fur le [...] le Roy [...] ſaigne al Roy [...]

Eynt Edward par la grce deu vist le ſour de paſk
al manger les .vii. dorman [...] deſtre coſtz ſur
[...]
kent [...] ngle de vn morſel. mult grnt mpra
[...] deu fur luy e [...] a vie e apres
[...] eruacion noſtre ſeignur .m. lxvi e de ſoen
reaume [...] euant ſa mort deuiſa ſeynt Edward
le reaume de Engelterre a William Baſtard ſoen neuou
adunkz dulz de Normundye. E puis mort ſeynt Ed
vard e gyſt enterrer a Weſtmuſter

11

country, for the prestige of the nation and, in due course, for preferment.

But the royal body is the same as every other physical body, and will get sick and swollen if it is subjected to such deluges of exotic foods. The king's personal appetite must be restrained and controlled if he is to maintain himself in good physical health. From the Middle Ages, the king had at his shoulder, at table, his own physician, advising him on the benefits or otherwise of the royal diet. It is for the sovereign to act on the doctor's advice. But the king acquires also a more ethereal being. His physical body, in the ritual of being crowned, has been secretly smeared with a sacred oil that has turned his person into God's anointed representative on earth; as James I said in 1609, 'even by God himself they are called gods'. This image of kingship was to lead to the civil wars of the seventeenth century, but even today something sets apart the anointed figure of majesty. Aside from its mystical significance, this body is also father or mother to the nation and figurehead of the country, and must fulfil this role, which regularly sees the sovereign sitting at the head of an overladen table, hosting a splendid banquet for world heads of state.

Throughout the history of the British Isles, crowned kings have struggled for and against grand rituals of communal dining. In Anglo-Saxon chronicles, fighting is more common than banqueting; on one occasion, king and soldiers were reduced to eating their own horses after the

Danes yet again plundered their stock and burned their crops. Even in a peaceful moment, more communal drinking than eating took place in the banqueting hall. Small wonder that the only culinary anecdote to survive is of Alfred burning the cakes, but then very few kings-in-waiting since have been equipped to boil an egg, let alone bake a cake.

Anglo-Saxons are depicted sailing, fighting or praying, never eating. Not until the reign of Edward the Confessor (1042–66) is the monarch shown at table (fig. 1). Already dishes are being offered on bended knee to the Christ-like figure at the table, which is covered, as an altar, with a white cloth. Then comes the disgrace of the ungoverned appetite of Henry I (1100–35), as every schoolchild knows even if he knows the meaning of neither 'lamprey' nor 'surfeit', resulting in the king's death.

By the time our story begins, in the fourteenth century, the ritual of royal dining was well established. By the end of the century, it was already being adapted for the comfort of the king, who desired some quiet meals away from the noisy bustle of the Great Hall. The battle for royal privacy and the requirement for the ritual of public royal dining would continue for centuries, as would the sovereign's conflict between his desire for health and longevity and his wish to tuck into all the magnificent dishes laid on his table.

Royal Bounty and the Land of Cockayne

'… *sometimes am I king;*
Then treasons make me wish myself a beggar,
And so I am …
I wasted time, and now doth time waste me'

William Shakespeare, *Richard II*, V. v

2. The aim of the subtlety was to combine magic and food – and to astonish. A peacock might be served in its plumage, or swans served swimming in pastry ponds. Real birds might even be hidden at the last moment in pies, to fly into the air as soon as the crust was cut.

Tall, blonde, deposed Richard II (1377–99), in the prime of his manhood at thirty-three, is about to take, or rather refuse, his final meal on earth. Prisoner of an unlawful king, Richard laments (in Shakespeare's words) his isolation in the keep of Pontefract Castle, 'Where no man never comes but that sad dog/That brings me food to make misfortune live' (V. v). Despite his desperate situation, Richard insists on the protocol of his kingship, commanding the keeper to taste his food before he eats, to which the keeper replies: 'My lord, I dare not.'

At this point in Shakespeare's play, the former king understands that he is being administered poison, and perhaps realizes fully the violation of his kingship and its rituals. He

attacks his guards and is run through with a sword. After his death his cousin, usurper of his throne and dining table, Henry Bolingbroke, now Henry IV (1399–1413), speaks the memorable line: 'They love not poison that do poison need' (V. vi).

Alternative accounts suggest that Richard either was starved to death in Pontefract Castle or, as Henry IV – in prose and not blank verse – declaimed, ended his life by refusing the sumptuous meals prepared for him in the prison kitchens. The truth, as so often, probably lies somewhere in between. Perhaps Richard fell prey to disease, his constitution weakened by a sparse and unaccustomed diet. At all events, he died within the walls of Pontefract

3. This image of Richard II in Westminster Abbey, painted on a wooden panel in the 1390s, is possibly by the court painter André Beauneveu, and is the earliest known portrait of an English monarch. After dinner the king would sit, enthroned, demanding obeisance from his knights.

4. Westminster Hall dates from the eleventh century. Richard II added the hammer-beam roof and twenty-six enchanting carved angels, which bear his arms entwined with those of Edward the Confessor. The hall provided the setting for Richard's coronation banquet and his deposition in 1399, and subsequently for coronation banquets for the next 420 years.

Castle in mid-February 1400, from causes unknown, but which all, to some degree, implicate food.

Richard of Bordeaux was born in 1367 into the court of Aquitaine, described by Jean Froissart as 'splendid and rich', and home of courtly love and chivalric values, to Joan, 'fair maid of Kent', and the legendary Black Prince. An elder brother died when Richard was five, and his father four years later; on the death of his grandfather Edward III (1327–77), Richard, aged ten, became King Richard II of England.

The child-king's coronation banquet, sketchily reported with little attention to the menu, took place in Westminster Hall (fig. 4). Finding more food on his trencher than appetite for it, Richard apparently drifted off to sleep, exhausted by the lengthy ritual of being crowned. Roused from his reverie by a loud hammering at the door and a fanfare of trumpets, Richard awoke to see the King's Champion galloping in full armour up to the top table, where he threw down his gauntlet, challenging to combat any man present who dared withhold allegiance to the new sovereign. The challenge going unanswered, the new king gave his champion a weighty gold cup for his efforts and retired to bed.

When Richard was fifteen, a bride arrived for him in the shapely form of Anne of Bohemia, the fifteen-year-old daughter of Charles IV, the Holy Roman Emperor. During

5. Richard II, beneath a
cloth of state, dines with
his uncles, the dukes of
York and Gloucester, and
his favourite, Robert de
Vere, Duke of Ireland.
One of the servants holds
a *nef*, an ornamental table
receptacle in the form of a
ship, used primarily by the
kings of France.

the twelve years of their joint rule, the young
couple established a scintillating court in
England. The late fourteenth century was both
the epitome and the valediction of the high
Middle Ages, with ladies in rich flowing gowns,
tall coned headdresses and floating, flimsy
veils. Men played at chivalry in the joust (a
colourful entertainment to accompany a
banquet) or, clad in particoloured skintight
leggings and long pointed shoes with tinkling
bells, sighed over troubadour tales of courtly

love. The early feminist writer Christine de
Pisan called Richard 'a true Lancelot', and he
was admired by the European intelligentsia
for his most un-English stance of being
flamboyantly dressed, cultured and a sensitive
gourmet. Richard's own cooks gave him the
title of 'the best and ryallest vyandier of all
christen kynges'.

Meanwhile the episodic Hundred Years
War rumbled on. Richard had little stomach
for warfare and no appetite for becoming a

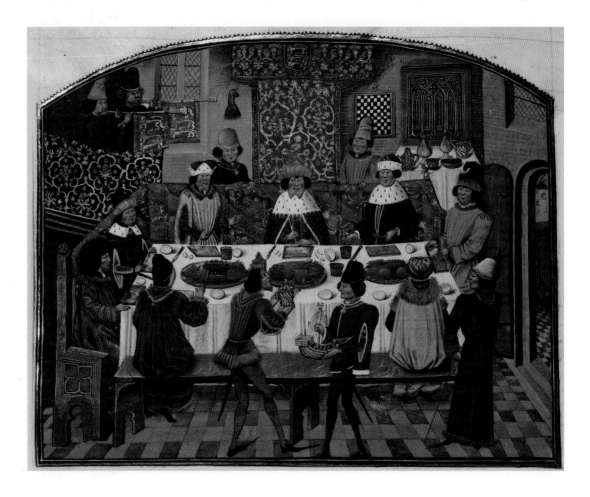

bloodthirsty Plantagenet in the footsteps of his romanticized father. The court was cleared of uncouth knights, lusting for battle, since Richard's tastes lay in art, poetry, food and fashion. His slender waist displayed leggings and jewelled surcoats to perfection, and he set the fashion. Men at court followed suit, becoming more practised in the bedchamber than on the battlefield, and although jousting was encouraged, Richard himself took no part. In this climate, the role of women at court was expanding, as was the range of foods, exotic and often Eastern-inspired, being placed on the courtiers' trenchers. Richard, from being addressed as 'my lord' by his close band of warmongering knights, now became 'Your Majesty' to the expanding household and the aristocracy, who were encouraged to attend his court. His Majesty began to take his meals alone in his chamber.

The severing of the bond of chummy eating with his knights was an excellent means of increasing the aloofness and aura of the king, and establishing his supremacy over the court. But it was also a dangerously isolating practice. Richard lost his means of hearing comradely dispute or careless complaints dropped from tipsy lips over a shared supper. When he did appear in the Great Hall, it was for a banquet, at which he was now the star attraction, seated alone under a canopy on the dais. A similar process was occurring in the courts of Paris and

Prague, and the subsidiary French and Italian courts. The European sovereign was becoming a man of letters and the pinnacle of fashion in all things, including food, feasting and table manners (fig. 6).

Richard was an extravagant host, although, on the occasion of Anne of Bohemia's entry into London for her coronation, he found the Exchequer coffers empty and was forced to borrow from a London grocer to rescue her crown from pawn and provide a welcoming banquet. At home, there were Christmas feasts at the royal palaces of Westminster, Sheen, Windsor Manor and Eltham, where Richard had just built a modern spicery and two sauceries. Tournaments with banquets were held. The king attended all, dressed throughout in full royal regalia, including his crown when he and Anne dined in state. There were dazzling receptions for foreign royalty – the Duke of Guelders, the King of Armenia – and dignitaries of the Church.

Richard II was himself richly entertained by those wishing to show their allegiance or gain royal favour. In September 1387 the Bishop of Durham held a magnificent banquet for the king and the Duke of Lancaster, in his London palace, to which some 2000 guests were invited. The shopping list opens with 1400 salted and 2 fresh oxen, 240 pigs, 120 sheep with their heads, 11,000 eggs and 120 gallons of milk, and includes more exotic fare, such as 50 swans,

6. Royal banquets became increasingly ostentatious throughout Europe during the course of the fourteenth century, although the prevalence of fish on the table in this image would suggest that this is a day of fasting. The king is being entertained by musicians as he eats.

144 whimbrel, 120 curlew, cranes, herons and bitterns. The king's own dinner consisted of three courses, each of ten dishes. It began with venison and frumenty, pottage, boars' heads, roast oxen, roast swan, roast pig and lumbardy custard; the second course included two thin pottages or soups, one called jelly, one white, as well as roast pigs and cranes, herons, pheasants, glazed and gilded chickens, bream, tarts, jellied brawn of deer and roast rabbits; and for the final course there was sweet soup with almonds, a honey, date and wine pudding, roast venison, roast chicken, rabbits, partridge, pigeons, quail, larks, pain puff (a type of puff pastry), jelly and long fritters (made with milk curds). Between courses, subtleties (see page 28) were displayed.

What appears to be a random assortment of mixed dishes in fact constitutes a well-designed menu for healthy eating, in accordance with the divinely regulated medieval system of the 'rule of four'. As there are four elements (earth, water, air and fire), four compass points and four seasons, so it was believed that there were four bodily and psychological states, known as the humours, which were governed by the qualities of the elements: dry, wet, cold and hot. Illness resulted from their imbalance in the body. A combination of warm and moist produced a sanguine temperament; warm and dry was choleric; cold and moist was phlegmatic; and cold and dry melancholic. Foods, classified in the same way, were important in balancing the

7. Melons being harvested in the early fifteenth century. Such soft fruit as plums, damsons and cherries was considered best eaten on an empty stomach. It was thought positively dangerous to eat a melon at any stage other than the very beginning of a meal.

to take pottage. Common sense and experience must also have been at work; some foods are harder to digest, some cause wind, and others are unsuitable during certain periods of life or poor at certain times of the year. If not fruit, pottage might prepare the stomach for the main course. Roasts – the most indigestible food – were served as a middle course, with pastries and pies to follow. At the end of a meal, pears, hard cheese and apples (considered an aid to digestion) were recommended, and finally a digestif, usually the spiced wine hippocras, with comfits, wafers and candied fruits. It was a brave cook who would serve his king strawberries and cream, which the early fifteenth-century guide *The Boke of Kervynge* (see page 24) asserted 'will make your soverayne sick', as would green salads and most raw fruit.

8. The cinnamon merchant. Spices were new to England in the Middle Ages, and many were thought to have medicinal or even magical properties. Cinnamon was believed to be found in the nest of the phoenix.

humours, but their characteristics could be tempered by the way they were prepared. Cold, moist fish could be fried, for example, or moist beef roasted (although some physicians considered beef to be dry, and suggested boiling it). Herbs and spices further assisted the balancing process. It was an esoteric science requiring professional interpretation.

The fourteenth-century recipe collection *The Forme of Cury* reports that the king's physician stood daily at his table, 'concelying his grace whyche dyet is best'. Richard II might be denied the roast beef he fancied and advised

9. A baker accused of giving short measure or selling bread made with rotten grain might be punished by being hauled through the town with a whetstone tied about his neck.

Many spices had been newly introduced from the Middle East by the returning Crusaders. Black pepper was thought to be guarded in its native India by fierce snakes, while grains of paradise, blown from trees, might be netted in the Nile. Rare and extremely expensive, spices were prized for their healing properties. Ginger was used to warm the stomach, aiding digestion; cloves to soothe the muscles; mace to control colic; and nutmeg to combat colds. Spices particularly favoured in winter were mustard, ginger, pepper, cloves and cinnamon, while herbs, lemon, pomegranate and verjuice (sour grape juice) were used as summer seasonings.

For king and court, hunting with dogs provided both sport and food for the table in the form of venison and wild boar. Hunting with falcons brought in pigeons and partridges; pheasants and rabbits were netted.

Large estates had their own ponds for breeding fish for the table. Sea fish and farmed meat were bought at market, as was dried fruit (such as dates and figs), spices and the new bitter oranges. There were penalties for selling food that was adulterated, in short measure or turning rotten. A butcher selling bad meat would have it burned under his nose as he sat in the stocks.

In the early 1390s there was money enough to fund Richard's grand banquets. Taxation had increased, and the king's enemies had been overcome, their lands and revenues seized by the crown. But in 1394 Queen Anne died of the plague, which over the course of the century had killed one-third of Europe's population, and a heartbroken Richard began to console himself with long drinking sessions, increasingly losing control of himself and his court.

In 1396 Richard was married again, to Isabelle, the daughter of Charles VI of France, but it was a dynastic alliance, a marriage in name only, his bride being but seven years old. During that decade the royal household grew to the unprecedented number of 500, increasing for brief periods to twice that size, and its annual expenditure doubled from £18,000 to £35,000. Its lavishness was such that a contemporary account reckoned Richard's kitchen staff to number 3000 and his court 10,000.

The household was organized into two distinct divisions. Richard's Lord Steward headed the *domus providencie,* comprising kitchen and stables. The kitchen was further divided into Buttery, with bakehouse and pantry, and Great Kitchen, with scullery, larders, spicery and a growing number of specialist offices. Purchasing comestibles and balancing the books were the responsibility of the Clerks of the Kitchen, whose ledgers were placed daily under the eyes of the ever-vigilant Cofferer. Ledgers gave details of food ordered, suppliers and prices. Good value and low cost were paramount. In the hot and noisy Great Kitchen, the king's Master Cook reigned supreme, issuing commands and experimenting with new dishes. A Master Cook who found a way to woo the royal stomach

10. As the king takes his place at table, the ewerer, a towel draped over his shoulder, is ready with a bowl of perfumed water for the preprandial washing of the royal hands.

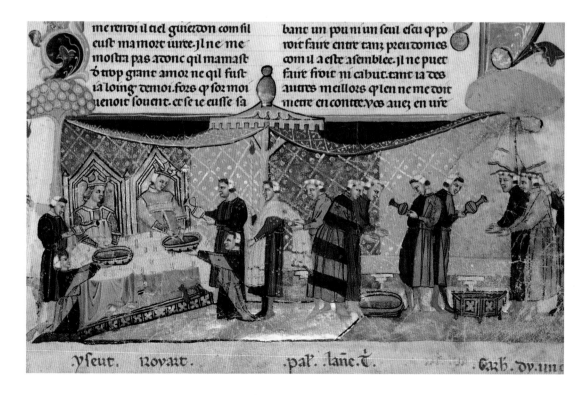

11. The pantler chopped, pared and squared slices of two-day-old bread to serve as plates, or trenchers. The king alone would be given a fresh trencher for each course. An uncouth chap who finished his meal by eating his gravy-soaked trencher, normally given to the poor, would be called a trencherman.

was sure to achieve eminence. The lowliest employees were the kitchen boys, who worked long hours turning spits, watching pots and running errands. The Master Cook himself had usually learned his trade in such humble employment, a fact that encouraged a twinkle of hope in the children's exhausted eyes. For an idle moment, they could dream of such a future for themselves, before the painful rap of the cook's basting spoon against the side of their heads returned them to the present.

Finished dishes were carried from the kitchen up to the Great Hall by liveried servants, accompanied with drum rolls and trumpet fanfares. To cries of 'Roome for my Lord's service. Gentlemen, Yeomen, waite on the Sewer', the usher led the sewer, or server, into the hall. The table was covered with three tablecloths, and the first item, the great salt, was placed to the right of the king's seat. The pantler, in charge of bread and salt, brought in fresh hot bread rolls wrapped in a cloth, and a pile of trenchers was set to the left of the salt, with the king's knife and spoon folded in a napkin. The whole was covered until his arrival. The king washed his hands, his chaplain said grace, then the three main servers – the sewer, the cupbearer and the carver – approached the king's table and bowed.

Every item of food and drink was first tested for poison. The king would choose from the dishes presented to him, sometimes in conference with his physician. On occasions of celebration, he was served by his best-loved knights, who must have appeared clumsy amateurs compared to his dexterous daily servers. The star turn at the king's table was undoubtedly the carver, whose fast-moving knife provided a flamboyant spectacle of poetry in motion.

Those in the main body of the hall received their food in messes, a helping designed usually to feed four. Men helped themselves and drank from a communal cup. Most brought their own knives, but they were provided with spoons and trenchers (fig. 11). At the end of the meal, the Almoner collected trenchers and leftovers into a *voyder*, or great basket, to be distributed to the poor, waiting at the gates. It was the usher's job to see that the best parts were not filched or merely thrown to the dogs.

John Russell's fifteenth-century *Boke of Nurture* offers instruction to a trainee pantler, chamberlain or carver, including how to

12. Fifteenth-century painting of a crab by Albrecht Dürer. Fish was the most difficult food to serve, since filleting was often required, although John Russell in his *Boke of Nurture* insists that a 'crabbe is a slutt to kerve'.

prepare appetizing sauces to make his noble lord 'glad and mery': mustard for brawn, beef and mutton; verjuice for boiled capon and veal; garlic for goose; and ginger for fawn. Russell was steward to Henry IV's son Humphrey of Gloucester, who was buried in a part of old St Paul's Cathedral subsequently named 'Duke Humphrey's Walk'. During the sixteenth century this became a place for beggars to congregate, so that 'dining with Duke Humphrey' came to mean 'no supper'. The early sixteenth-century *Boke of Kervynge*, printed by Wynken de Worde, provided further instruction, including forty picturesque ways of carving flesh: 'batache that cuclewe; lyste that swanne; spatre that pyke and baderttraunche that purpose [porpoise]'.

Throughout the meal, the butler was on hand, mixing wine for the king and checking that no substandard drinks were poured for the cupbearer to serve. The wine was also tasted to ensure that no poison had been added. Wines from Bordeaux were the favourite of the English court; grapes were grown in England, but their wine was considered poor. According to a twelfth-century scholar, a good wine should be as clear as 'the tears of a penitent'. The common man's drink was ale, sometimes new and cloudy, but consumed with relish and in great quantity. Made from malted barley, it was a nutritious drink. Hops were later added, making beer, which kept for longer but was thought to aggravate kidney stones and colic.

Images from the early fifteenth century show dishes for the Duke of Berry being taken from a credenza, or sideboard, alongside the table (fig. 13). Originally a useful station for pouring wine and storing tableware, this gradually became a showplace for displaying the family silver. At the royal table, gold and silver plates replaced the humble trencher.

On the French royal table, the most prominent piece of silverware was the *grand nef*, which, as its name implies, was usually in the form of a ship. It was principally a mark of wealth and status, although it also served as a receptacle for anything from serpents' tongues (as sharks' teeth were known; these were said to sweat or change colour in the presence of poison) to gold spoons or damask napkins. *Nefs* were rarely seen in England, where kings favoured the great salt as an ostentatious centrepiece (fig. 14).

Gold cups, or *hanaps*, were popular New Year gifts between monarchs. In 1396 at Ardres,

13. The Duke of Berry, brother of Charles V of France, dines in royal style. There is an ostentatious *nef* on his table, and on the far left a credenza, or sideboard, is piled high with gold and gilt dishes.

14. Louis XI's Great Salt was made of gold, pearls and jasper. Richard II possessed many great salts, all of which were melted down at his death. One was in the form of a hart, the king's emblem, while another, made from jasper, was said to sweat in the presence of poison.

Richard II presented Charles VI and the Duke of Berry with gilt cups and ewers. The French king returned the compliment, presenting Richard with an exquisite gilt *nef* carved with a tiger on the prow and stern. It went the way of many such items, being pawned to pay English soldiers in the ongoing wars with France. Similarly, Richard II's collection of some 200 gold, jewelled and enamelled cups was melted down at his death to pay off debts.

It was during the reign of Richard II that the first cookbook in England came into being. *The Forme of Cury* (or 'The Method of Cooking') contains almost 200 recipes and was written on a 20-foot-long vellum roll by the king's Master Cooks, with comments from the 'Maisters of Phisik and of Philosophie that dwellid in his court'. At the time of the book's appearance, in about 1390, a lull was taking place in what we now call the Hundred Years War, but the language of warfare seems to infiltrate every page, with 'hewing', 'smiting him to pecys', 'spoiling', 'splatting', 'seething', scalding, mincing, grinding and shredding much in evidence. This might give the impression, as it did to Samuel Pegge, the editor of the eighteenth-century version, that *The Forme of Cury*'s recipes 'are chiefly soups, pottages, ragouts, hashes … and animals, whether fish or fowl, seldom brought to table whole, but hacked and hewed, and cut in pieces or gobbets'. However, as we have seen, the art

15. Gathering spinach. An easy-growing early spring vegetable newly arrived in fourteenth-century England from Spain, 'spynoches' was an instant favourite. *The Forme of Cury* suggests parboiling it and frying in olive oil with sweetened cinnamon and nutmeg – a dish likely to appeal to the refined taste of Richard II.

of the carver was highly skilled and consisted in far more than hacking food into 'gobbets' or dishing up pap. The recipes in the book, many collated from earlier sources, range from simple fritters, chicken in gravy and meat pies to rich tagine-like mixtures of fruit, meat and spices. Anything caught in the sea, such as porpoises, or that flew in the sky, such as bitterns, curlews and swans, might end up on the king's table. The book contains Italian recipes, including *loseyns* (lasagne) cooked in spiced broth with grated cheese; mouth-numbingly horrendous recipes, such as 'newe noumbles' of deer (entrails boiled in salted water); and such soothing dishes as blancmange and white chicken.

16. Frontispiece to Taillevent's late fourteenth-century cookbook *Le Viandier*, which was a huge success. The poet François Villon, in his bestselling *Grand Testament* (1461), lauded its fricassées. *Le Viandier* retained its appeal until the beginning of the seventeenth century, becoming, by the bye, the bingeing bible of the budding bourgeoisie.

Possibly not by coincidence, *The Forme of Cury* appeared ten years after the French cookbook *Le Viandier* (fig. 16). This was written by Guillaume Tirel, known as 'Taillevent', chief cook to the French kings Charles V and Charles VI (fig. 17). Tirel had worked his way up in the French royal kitchens from lowly spit-turner to the top job of *Grand Queux de France* (Superintendent of the King's Kitchens). Interestingly, the French Master Cook's name is known to us, while his English counterparts remain anonymous. In France, cooks were feted and treasured, lent, borrowed and even stolen.

Whereas *The Forme of Cury* barks orders, *Le Viandier* hints and suggests: perhaps half to

17. Taillevent, 'première vedette de la gastronomie', rose from kitchen boy to king's cook. He died wealthy and lies in a stately tomb at St Germain-en-Laye on the outskirts of Paris, with a wife on each marble arm and a shield bearing his coat of arms, which features three hefty cooking pots.

an ounce of ginger to a pint of sauce? Taste it and see. *Le Viandier* speaks as a friend to an experimenting cook; the English book dictates as though cooking were a necessity, but hardly a pleasure. Cooking methods were limited and ingredients differed little between the two countries, but the French version already says 'food is good, prepare with care – and enjoy it'.

The appreciation of food in the fourteenth-century court involved all the senses; an early objection to the fork, for example, was its interference with the direct processes of touch and taste. Paramount, however, was the impression given to the eye. The great royal banquet demanded a showpiece – the 'subtlety' – which could be served between courses while the tables were being cleared and when a pause to digest the rich food was required. Original subtleties might have been simply a gilded dish of coloured frumenty (a sweet porridge made of wheat flavoured with cinnamon). The idea was developed to add magic, mystery and surprise to the meal, and food was made to appear other than it was. Cooked animals could be made to look alive, and lifelike sculptures were created in marchpane (marzipan, but with more nuts than in today's version) or spun sugar. There was the Cockentrice, an eccentric dish created by sewing the head of a piglet on to the body of a capon. The aim with all subtleties was to provoke a cry of surprise and delight (fig. 2).

18. In 1378 the Holy Roman Emperor (Richard II's father-in-law) was feted by his nephew, the French king Charles V, in Paris at a magnificent feast in which the 'entremets', or inter-course entertainment, consisted of a small-scale re-enactment of the Crusaders' capture of Jerusalem.

19. During a banquet entertainment in 1393, five dancers, including Charles VI of France, caught fire. Four of the king's knights were burned to death, and the king was saved only by the quick-thinking Duchess of Berry, who threw her gown over him, extinguishing the flames.

20. An acorn-fattened pig is dispatched for the Christmas feast. No part of the pig will be wasted, and he will continue to feed the family throughout the year, an insurance against bad harvests and unsuccessful snaring. A woman stands by with a bowl for the blood.

Such entertainments quickly became increasingly extravagant. Model castles were filled with sugar knights, and gardens contained edible trees bearing miniature candied fruits and gilded fountains from which the finest wines flowed. Gradually, subtleties developed into a form of entertainment in their own right. Painted scenery prompted the re-enactment of glorious events; and minstrels, troubadours and jongleurs performed (fig. 18).

A disastrous entertainment took place in France in 1393, when Charles VI and four of his knights dressed up as wild men in tight-fitting linen suits, soaked in resin and stuck with shaggy hair. They performed an uninhibited dance, which got out of hand when one of the dancers went too near a flaming torch and fire engulfed them all (fig. 19).

Fun and games were not always the order of the day. The Church had decreed as early as AD 325 that the forty days before Easter should be kept as a fast. This was extended in 1253 to make a total of 242 days of the year when meat, and sometimes also dairy products and eggs,

Il vient dire et maudit sa vie et toute sa generacion et ilz vont tout aper biacon.

21. The poor and hungry of Europe united in a vision of a land of plenty – this was the land of Cockayne – where roasted geese flew through the air and every appetite was effortlessly satiated.

was excluded from the diet. Fish – which did not copulate and were thus immune from the sin of sexual indulgence – were allowed. Barnacle geese were considered fish because nobody knew where they came from, as were beavers, which had fish-like tails. The rich paid with penance money for the privilege of eating forbidden food on fast days. With money raised in this way the gourmet citizens of Rouen rebuilt the tower of their church,

and it still goes by the name of the Butter Tower.

Above pride and next to sex, gluttony – which encompassed overeating, overdrinking, eating before grace, eating without appetite, gobbling and not giving a share to the poor – constituted a mortal sin. A lecherous mouth had a lecherous tail. Overtaxed peasants rarely got a taste of this delectable evil, of course. The lords at the top table were overburdened with choice, but those at the bottom ate their way through a diet that changed only with the seasons. For them, Lent meant switching from salted bacon to pickled herrings, and Christmas meant pork and ale. At the thin end of the year, herbs and roots might be all that was available to put into the pot. In the 1370s and 1380s there were riots across Europe as taxes rose and harvests were poor. Those tempted to supplement their diet with a little game could be executed or have a hand chopped off for poaching, although hares and rabbits might be trapped – if any remained after the king's men had taken their share.

Court leftovers were available to those desperate enough to spend hours waiting at the palace gates. Many must have dreamed of the warm fire in the Great Hall and the tables piled high with roast meat, game, custards, soups, fried fish, fritters and jellies – the vision a poet relates in the story of Sir Gawain and the Green Knight, when

King Arthur lay at Camelot upon a Christmas-tide, with many a gallant lord and lovely lady …

Then they bare the first course, with the blast of trumpets and the waving of banners, with the sound of drums and pipes, of song and lute, that many a heart was uplifted at the melody. Many were the dainties, and rare the meats, so great was the plenty they might scarce find room on the board to set on the dishes. Each helped himself as he liked best, and to each two were twelve dishes, with great plenty of beer and wine.

To the hungry hordes not invited to the feast came a vision of plenty – the land of Cockayne – where all their wants would be satisfied. King Richard II might have been better advised to invite some of the starving poor to his feasts, rather than his own kith and kin who were already plotting against him. He had been warned by an astrologer that a toad would bring about his downfall, and when his cousin, Henry Bolingbroke, strode into the king's hall for the Christmas banquet wearing a robe embroidered with images of toads, Richard might have reflected on his misspent time, for his final meal in Pontefract Castle already beckoned.

Tudor 'Banketynge Braynlesse' in England and France

'Wine is but single broth,
Ale is meat, drink and cloth.'
Sixteenth-century saying

22. Detail from *The Field of Cloth of Gold* by an unknown artist, *c.* 1545. Outside the timber 'palace' at Guisnes, two ornate fountains flowed with wine. They inevitably attracted local layabouts, who soon lay about them in great drunken heaps and had to be removed on pain of being hanged.

June: gloriously long, hot days, balmy scented evenings and the first sweet strawberries of the season – the perfect time for a French camping holiday and picnics. That can hardly be what Henry VIII (1509–47), or more probably Thomas Wolsey, the king's first minister, had in mind when the idea was floated of a summit meeting in 1520 with the friendly foe across the channel, François I of France. But its spin-offs were the most magnificent campsites ever pitched and the most extraordinarily lavish picnic food ever prepared. Those who witnessed the event were able to dine out on it for the rest of their lives, although the resulting peace treaty fell apart in less time than it took to get back to England (fig. 23).

Two highly ambitious, upwardly mobile families erect their tents in neighbouring plots; to be friendly, the wife has the man of the other family over to dinner, while her husband is entertained by the other camper's family. Each is, above all, hell-bent on impressing his neighbour. That was what happened at the Field of Cloth of Gold, but on a much grander scale. Being kings, Henry and François were able to spend unlimited money on provisions; to throw in jousting, tournaments, wrestling, archery, fireworks, banquets, masques and dancing, instead of barbecues, rounders and beach cricket, by way of entertainment; and to offer diamond-and-ruby rings, instead of a bottle of plonk, when they came to dinner. Both

23. Detail from *The Field of Cloth of Gold* by an unknown artist, *c.* 1545. The procession of the English party, with Henry VIII and his first minister, Cardinal Wolsey, arrives at Guisnes.

kings were in their twenties, and both were intent on overwhelming the other with their regal magnificence, their wealth, their power and their physical prowess (figs. 24 and 25).

The English overreached themselves, fashioning 'great and goodlie pavilions' (according to Exchequer accounts) from cloth of gold (woven with gold and silver thread), with poles decorated with gilded vanes of the king's beasts – lion, dragon, greyhound and antelope. The interiors they dressed with tapestries, rich damask hangings, velvet and silk. Both nations tried to prepare their tents in secret. The French sent out spies, who reported that the English were making bigger, better

and more opulent tents; the English spies came back with a similar message. At Ardres, François unwisely made his principal tent, which was lined with blue velvet sprinkled with gold fleurs-de-lys, so tall – 120 feet – that its pole snapped in the strong winds that, with 'rains and thunder', plagued the midsummer of 1520, disrupting the jousting and covering so much cloth of gold with dust.

Five miles down the road, inside the English pale at Guisnes, Henry built a 30-foot-high crenellated timber palace on brick foundations with huge glass windows (5000 square feet of glass was used) and a tarpaulin roof painted to resemble tiles

24. Young Henry VIII by Joos van Cleve, *c.* 1535: a Renaissance prince in his prime. He was fond of food, music, poetry, sport and, of course, women.

25. François I of France by Jean Clouet, *c.* 1530. François, king of France for five years, was twenty-five, and Henry VIII, king for eleven years, was twenty-eight at the time of the Field of Cloth of Gold. Great similarities and rivalry existed between the two men, who died within eight weeks of each other in 1547.

(fig. 22). In common with the French king, Henry had a cloth-of-gold dining tent with a privy kitchen, but there was neither time nor materials to build the intended banqueting house. Wood was in short supply in Calais, and timber had to be floated down by sea from The Netherlands.

The English purchased 216,000 gallons of wine, mostly from Burgundy and the Rhine valley, along with the sweet wines so popular in England, and seventy tuns or large casks of ale and beer, the total cost of which was over £1500. But in any case Henry normally spent £3000 a year, a tenth of his annual income, on drink. The English already had a reputation

on the Continent as hard drinkers. However, what really shocked the French at the Cloth of Gold tournaments were what John Fisher, Bishop of Rochester, described as 'fayre ladyes in sumptuouse and gorgeouse apparel' in the galleries, who behaved like ladettes, swigging wine from a large flask that they passed around among themselves, while loudly cheering on their team. This assembly of inebriated females did most certainly not include the reserved Queen Katherine, although watching from among the horrified French court may well have been a nineteen-year-old English girl by the name of Anne Boleyn, whose elder sister Mary was part of the English retinue.

26. Wine being imported from Bruges. 'All the kyngdomes of the worlde have not so many sundry kyndes of wynes, as be in Englande and yet is nothynge to make wyne of' (Andrew Boorde, 1490–1549).

Enormous quantities of food had been obtained from every possible source. The estates of England were hunted for deer, grain was emptied from every store, the seas were trawled and all manner of birds shot from the skies. The historian Edward Hall reported in about 1550 that 'forestes, parkes, felde, salt seas, ryvers, moates and pondes were searched … for the delicacie of viandes, well was that man rewarded that could bring any thinge of lykinge or pleasure.' One man who came up with the goods was William Wolverston, the king's sea-fisher. He managed to catch 5 dories, 48 mullets, 21 bass, 30 turbots, 9100 plaice,

7836 whiting, 6 halibuts, 700 conger eels, 488 cod, 5554 soles, 1 dolphin, 300 bream, 1890 mackerel, 3 porpoises, 11 haddock, 3 crabs, 1 lobster, 4 trout, 2800 crayfish, 1 fresh sturgeon and 3 fresh salmon. For this trawl, he was rewarded with a sum approaching £1500.

Orders for the Acatery, responsible for purchasing livestock, listed 373 oxen, 2014 mutton at 3s. 7d. each, 852 veals, 18 'hogs of grease', 51 pigs, 16 lambs and 101 'flitches' or sides of bacon. Further consignments of coastal fish were purchased: flounders, roach (3300), rudd, carp, eels, crabs, lobster and ling. Another bill came in for £1500. The poultry order included the usual hens (492), pullets (331), capons (1261), geese (506), quails (3000) and pheasants (82); the irregular numbers would lead one to suppose that as many were delivered as could be supplied. In addition, more exotic birds were on the menu: peacocks (2), gulls (199), cygnets (92), storks (78), herons (632), shovellers (65) and bitterns (86), along with whimbrels, egrets and curlews. Some 30,700 eggs, 2165 rabbits and 12 kid were added. Finally, 241 lb of butter at 2d./lb, 432 gallons of cream, 946 gallons of curd and 562 gallons of milk completed this order, which again added up to £1500 – perhaps a preset limit.

A thousand pippin apples, half as many oranges, 200 lemons, 16 lb of capers, olives and 34 gallons of oil are also listed in the accounts,

27. Giuseppe Arcimboldo, *L'Eau*, 1566. Fish was eaten on the many days meat was forbidden by the Church. Dolphin, porpoise, turbot, seal and sturgeon were considered fish fit for a king, regularly appearing on Henry VIII's table during Lent and other days of fasting.

28. Cornelis Jacobsz. Delff,
Still Life of Kitchen Utensils,
c. 1600. The weight of the
pewter dishes transported
to France for the event
known as the Field of
Cloth of Gold was
estimated at over 10,000 lb.
In addition, skimmers,
ladles and giant mixing
bowls were required, and
a great kettle for boiling
beef.

although very few vegetables appear. They were certainly on the menu, but were probably locally sourced. In fact, carriage was a great problem and a further expense. Birds, for example, travelled in cages and were slaughtered just before being cooked.

In addition, the makeshift camp-kitchens had to be fitted out, not with utility camping gear, but with all the equipment needed for making and serving complicated dishes and sophisticated sauces for several hundred top-drawer guests. They required solid silver dishes and gold plates for serving up to the kings; only silver-gilt was required for queens.

Some of the items being transported were extremely fragile. The Windsor Herald had thirty-nine boxes made in which to convey the subtleties. Sadly, these decorations are not described, although their estimate in the accounts at 14*d.*/lb means they were probably constructed from sugar or marzipan in the form of fabulous heraldic beasts or figures from legend. Hercules was always a good metaphor for a king, and one used on this occasion by Henry (see page 42). The sugar sculptor may have captured the hero's labours or, using marchpane, fashioned a model of one of the king's castles. (Wolsey was to create an

amazing display of subtleties, about 100 in number, at a dinner he gave at Hampton Court in 1527 for the French ambassadors, of which 'the French men never saw the like'. According to George Cavendish, a gentleman usher in Wolsey's entourage, 'a chess board subtly made of spiced sweetmeat, with men of the same' so enchanted one of the visiting ambassadors that a case was made for it, so he could take it home with him.) Crates, too, were required to take to France the great bowls for serving hippocras. English expenditure for the twenty-day event had reached a total of £8839. 2*s.* 4*d*., in a year when the average labourer was earning less than 11*d*. a day.

The first banquets were held (fig. 29). One for François, in the tapestry-hung 'palace' at Guisnes, was hosted by Queen Katherine,

Mary, Duchess of Suffolk and Cardinal Wolsey. The other, for Henry VIII, took place at Ardres, in a tent hung with cloth of gold, hosted by the very pregnant twenty-year-old Queen Claude and her mother-in-law, Louise de Savoie. The French tables were decorated with subtleties representing leopards, salamanders and ermines, and the food was carried in great procession by liveried servants. Cannon sounded as each king left his lodgings, as the French note-taker had it, to ensure that each was hostage for the other.

The English certainly had quantity and variety on their side in the food they dished up to the French: the menu included soup, boiled capon, kid, cygnets, baked venison, pike, fritters, pear pies, custard, apples, sturgeon, peacock, pigeon, quail, wrens, baked venison, storks, pheasant, gulls, chicken, egrets, marrow bones, bream, oranges, baked meats … In fact, the foods cooked by the English and the French were probably similar, although it was simply noted that 'the French king was served three courses and his meat dressed after the French fashion and the King of England had the like after the English fashion'. The main dishes were spectacular, designed primarily to impress the eye. Peacock Royale, where the bird was served with its feathers on and with its beak gilded, was a favourite of kings, as was roast swan. Asparagus, a new arrival, would have been much in demand, and, to add a

lighter touch, there were salads decorated with midsummer flowers. The expense of the food ordered cannot yet have made much of a dent in the Exchequer, but it was making quite an impression on the region surrounding the encampment. The area around Calais was running out of both meat and fuel. It was recorded that by the time of the final banquet, if not before, the kings and queens dined privately in advance, and just admired the array of dishes and the ambience. It must have been disheartening for the cooks, but banquet fatigue had set in.

On Sunday 24 June, the final day of the Field of Cloth of Gold, François rode to Guisnes in disguise, with about twenty of his entourage. The men wore masks, and the ladies were dressed romantically in the 'old Italian style', with veiled, horned headdresses. Queen Katherine was used to this infantile kind of practical joke, which was frequently played on her by her husband, who adored arriving supposedly incognito. She pretended not to recognize François – rather like an eight-year-old indulging her father in his Santa Claus outfit. After he had changed back into his regal magnificence, the queen expressed the required amazement and presented the king with a diamond-and-ruby ring for his superb performance in the lists. At the same time, Henry VIII was on his way to Ardres disguised as Hercules, to inflict similar jesting pain on Queen

30. Detail from *The Field of Cloth of Gold* by an unknown artist, *c.* 1545. It was a tour de force to put together the kitchens and equipment, under awnings, let alone the amount of food and the disciplined order for its production and exquisite presentation. It would have taxed the most able chef with his own team in his familiar kitchens.

Claude, from whom he received two diamond-and-ruby rings for his part in the joust. The two kings crossed paths on the way back and spent an hour amicably chatting, parting with good heart and many gifts – although Henry most certainly did not disclose to François that he had a meeting lined up with the Emperor on his way home to England. Within two years France and England would once again be at war.

So, if not political, did the Field of Cloth of Gold serve any purpose at all? It certainly provided one of the greatest spectacles of the sixteenth century, but it must have bankrupted many people for the rest of their lives and beyond. Fisher preached several months later about the vanity of it all. He spoke of the winds that blew away the 'houses buylded for pleasure', and the dust that encompassed all

31. This highly ornate silver-gilt Royal Clock Salt was presented to Henry VIII as a New Year gift by François I in 1535. It is one of only three of Henry VIII's 2000 items of plate to survive.

silks, velvets and cloth of gold, righteously ending with the useful comments that the cloth 'cometh onely off the poore shepes backes' and the 'sylkes' from the 'intrales of wormes'; that the difference between an emperor and a poor man lies in precious stones and richness of apparel alone. For expressing the less radical notion that the king's divorce was against the law of God, he would, fifteen years later, lose his head.

Two years on, in 1522, England was an open ally of the Emperor and enemy of the French. What the French really thought about English food comes out when politeness retreats and a normal state of warfare is resumed. The poet Clément Marot wrote a few lines from the French to the English, which had been expressed frequently before and have been reiterated many, many more times since: 'Retirez vous arrière/ angloys désordonnez/ et buvez vostre bière/ Mengez vos beufz sallez' (Get back, you English rabble, to your beer and [dirty] salted beef).

The English satirist John Skelton had summed up the Field of Cloth of Gold in 1521: 'There hath ben moche excesse/ With banketynge braynlesse,/ With ryotynge rechelesse/ With gambaudynge [gambolling] thryftlesse,/ With, 'spende', and wast witlesse,/ Treatinge of trewse restlesse,/ Pratynge for peace peaslesse./ The countrynge at Cales/ Wrang us on the males [purses]!' All hope of

32. From the 1530s, when the king was in residence, between 600 and 1000 members of his court would eat twice daily, in two sittings, at tables in the Great Hall at Hampton Court Palace.

33. While lower-ranking members of the court dined in the Great Hall, senior courtiers ate in the Great Watching Chamber next door. This imaginary view, created by Joseph Nash in the nineteenth century, shows Cardinal Wolsey dining with his household in the Great Watching Chamber at Hampton Court.

34. Henry VIII is depicted dining in his Privy Chamber in a sixteenth-century drawing by Hans Holbein the Younger. The king eats alone, under a canopy of state. To his left is a dresser displaying his wealth of plate.

peace and prosperity was dispersed in the wind; there were only the bills left to pay.

Back in England, Henry VIII moved with the seasons between his large palaces of Greenwich, Eltham, Whitehall, Richmond and sometimes Windsor, with occasional nights in a variety of lesser manor houses and lodges. From 1528 he became especially fond of Hampton Court Palace, newly built by and acquired from Wolsey. The king was enriching this already splendid building with magnificent new additions, which included greatly extending its kitchens and offices to an area of 36,000 square feet, for the service not primarily of the king but of his court (figs. 35 and 36).

The king's meals were prepared for him by his own French chef in the Privy Kitchen, near his private apartments. The ritual of formal royal dining had changed little since the time of Richard II. The king took his seat in his chamber under a canopy of state (fig. 34). His servers dressed the table with cloths, a great salt, silver plate, his knife and spoon and a manchet or bread roll wrapped in a napkin. The dishes were offered by servers on bended knee, and almost anything the king could wish for was likely to be on the menu.

Lenten diets began to be phased out in England after Henry VIII's break with the Roman church in 1534. Four years later, the king issued a proclamation that the nation need no longer observe the Lenten fast, because, he was informed, of a scarcity of fish. Fish – a permitted food, as we have seen – had previously been abundant, at least on the king's table, during the many fasting days of the Church calendar. A fast meal served to Henry VIII and Katherine of Aragon in 1526, for example, included a first course of soup, herring, cod, lampreys, pike, salmon, whiting, haddock, plaice, bream, porpoise, seal, carp, trout, crabs, lobsters, custard, tart, fritters and fruit. This was followed by a second course of soup, sturgeon, carp, perch, eels with roast lampreys, shrimps, tarts, fritters, oranges, apples and baked eggs. The meal may have followed Church doctrine to the letter, but it was hardly a fast.

35. The Tudor kitchens at Hampton Court Palace. Serving hatches were placed at the east end of Cardinal Wolsey's great kitchen and held open, according to the Exchequer accounts, by 'iii houcks of irne'. From here, hot dishes were carried by liveried servants up the back stairs to courtiers dining in the Great Hall and the Great Watching Chamber.

36. Joints of meat were roasted on spits in front of the great log fire. Gentler cooking was done on charcoal ranges, and meat for stews and pies was simmered in the large copper boiler in the boiling house or in smaller cauldrons hung over the fire. Pastry was baked in the pastry office ovens.

During Lent the king's servants were on the whole served a healthier but unvarying diet of brown bread (known as 'cheat'), ale, herrings and salt cod. Fresh fish was always available for the king at Hampton Court Palace from the breeding ponds alongside its south gardens. Vegetables are not much mentioned in the court diet, although a new kitchen garden was made at Hampton Court in 1537, growing onions, leeks, cabbages, peas, beans, salads and herbs. It was beside the orchard, which was planted with apple, pear, damson and cherry trees. Katherine of Aragon was fond of oranges from her native Spain, and Henry, too, was fond of fruit, particularly pears, apples, plums and damsons. The queen introduced

marmalade, a thick orange or apricot jelly. Cherries and strawberries were more to the taste of the king's second wife, the ill-fated Anne Boleyn (fig. 38). Their shared sweet tooth may have prompted Henry to build a banqueting house in his Privy Garden at Hampton Court. A pretty little house, it stood on a mount and had great windows on all sides giving views over the river and the park. It was accessed by a winding path bordered with fragrant plants, and had its own kitchen down a spiral staircase. It was surely conceived for dalliances on summer evenings, for toying with newfangled forks and popping sweetmeats into the rosy mouth of the king's new love, the fair Anne. Their daughter, Elizabeth, would inherit that sweet tooth and love of banqueting. However, Henry and Anne's intertwined badges were still being painted on the door and the onion-dome roof gilded as Anne was shipped down the river in 1536 to be executed in the Tower of London.

Henry married his third wife, Jane Seymour, soon afterwards. In 1537, during the early stages of Jane's pregnancy, she developed a taste for fat quail. When she had eaten her way through those to be found at Dover and Calais, messengers were sent with all speed to Flanders to bring back more birds. Perhaps those extra snacks were instrumental in producing the much longed-for son in October of that year.

37. Cooks in the kitchens at Hampton Court Palace follow Tudor menus and methods of cooking. The cook in the foreground is making the pastry for pies using the pork filling in the bowl. The cook in the background is adding ingredients to a beef stew simmering on a charcoal stove.

38. Strawberries were prized in the sixteenth century for their sweetly scented leaves, and the fruits were a favourite with Henry VIII and Anne Boleyn.

39. Watercolour by Jacques Le Moyne de Morgues, 1568. Henry VIII encouraged his gardeners to grow tender Mediterranean vegetables, such as artichokes, and exotic fruits, including apricots, in the gardens of his new palace at Nonsuch in Surrey.

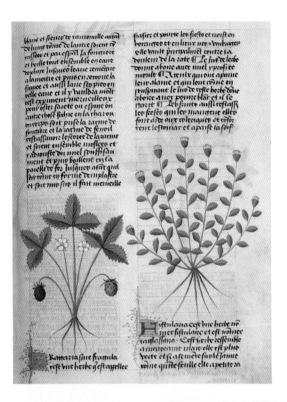

40. Rabbits, or conies, had been bred in the grounds at Hampton Court since the fourteenth century. They were hunted, and almost certainly poached, for both meat and fur.

41. Charles Brandon, Duke of Suffolk, was Lord Steward from 1540 to 1545. Only three men, all of high rank, filled this office during the reign of Henry VIII. Brandon married the king's sister, Mary.

Even with the addition of vegetables and the deprivations of Lent, the main fare for king and court was meat – and lots of it. Beef, mutton and pork were popular, as were geese, chickens, the newly introduced turkeys, swans, peacocks, curlews, storks and bitterns. Deer and game birds were hunted for the table in extensive parklands by king and court, when in season, as were conies, or rabbits (fig. 40). Sweet and savoury dishes were enhanced with sugar and spice if they were destined for the king's table. Otherwise salt was the most widely used seasoning, adding not only to the flavour but also to the preservation of meat and fish.

With the great quantity of provisions moving into, around and out of the palaces, an efficient system was required to avoid both waste and embezzlement. Instructions for the running of the royal household had been set down in the fifteenth century in the so-called Black Book, which Wolsey updated at Eltham Palace in 1525 and which became known as the Eltham Ordinances. Their aim was one of reform and retrenchment in many areas, including the purchase, storage, preparation, distribution and serving of food. Procedures were streamlined by the introduction of specialist storage areas and orderly deliveries to the Master Cook and his team of twelve cooks in the main kitchen. The 200 staff working in the kitchens at Hampton Court were all men, apart

Domus Prouidentiæ.

42. At Hampton Court, the room used by the Board of Green Cloth overlooks the courtyard where provisions were unloaded. Clerks made spot checks of comestibles arriving and leaving the palace, as well as of items stored in the large number of kitchen offices.

from 'the wife that makes the king's puddings' in the Confectionery. These skilled workers accompanied the king from palace to palace. In smaller residences, where the whole court could not be accommodated, the kitchen staff was proportionately reduced.

Lists were drawn up of those entitled to 'Bouche of Court', or the right to eat at the king's expense. For them, two meals a day were provided in the Great Hall at 10 am and 4 pm, each in two sittings (fig. 32). A daily allowance of bread, wine, beer, candles and firewood was also provided. In addition to those receiving the ordinary Bouche of Court was a small number of courtiers of higher standing, who ate apart in the Great Watching Chamber (fig. 33). As their status dictated, their dishes were more varied and plentiful than the standard 'messes' served up in the Great Hall.

At the head of this very busy department of the royal household was the Lord Steward (fig. 41). Almost invariably a nobleman, and often an intimate of the king, he wielded great power and influence at court, also sitting in judgement in his own court on any of the king's servants found disobeying instructions. The day-to-day running of the household below stairs was undertaken by the Board of Green Cloth. This was made up of the body of accountants, and was named after the green baize cloth of the table around which they sat to hold daily meetings, making calculations

43. The young Henry VIII led an active life, but after a joust wound to his leg, his activities were curtailed, his temper became uncertain and his weight escalated. Charles Laughton, in the film *The Private Life of Henry VIII* (1933), eats in an uncouth manner that would have horrified the real king.

44. A German woodcut of 1540 shows a cook at work in his well-stocked kitchen. There was piped spring water at Hampton Court Palace, and cleanliness was expected in the kitchens.

with lead tally counters and recording their transactions on rolls. These provide us today with information about what was ordered in the kitchens, from whom, and how much money was paid out (fig. 42). At the head of this table sat the Cofferer, who was in charge of the coffers and of accounting to the Exchequer how the money had been spent. Liaising with the Board of Green Cloth was the Clerk of the Kitchen, who planned the menus with the Master Cook and ordered provisions at the best price he could obtain. The king's men were in a favourable position in the marketplace, since they had a right of requisition when certain foods were in short supply. The Eltham Ordinances as implemented by the Board of Green Cloth were extremely efficient and, in a degenerate form, were still in operation in the royal household at the end of the eighteenth century.

Another method of retrenchment of royal household expenditure was used regularly by Henry VIII's younger daughter, Elizabeth, during her long and expensive reign (1558–1603): going to stay with one's friends. Royal visits encouraged the aristocracy to rearrange their bedchambers and queue up for the privilege of entertaining her, although they bankrupted many of her hosts. Banqueting houses aplenty were built as the nobility of England threw sovereign after sovereign in the attempt to woo the Virgin Queen.

In the sixteenth century one was expected to leave one's 'manners' behind when at the table. It was the correct thing to do, 'manners' being what was left on the plate, which was, in turn, what fed the poor man at the gate. As for behaviour at table, the advice given in the *Babees' Book* (1475) to young boys about to enter the service of a noble lord or prince still held good. It was relevant both to children

and to those adults who had yet to learn the rules of polite eating, and remains remarkably similar to the advice given to children today:

> *Wash your hands before you eat,*
> *Don't let the children linger at the table,*
> *Don't fart,*
> *Don't pick your nose, your teeth or any part*
> *   of your body when at table,*
> *Don't wipe your hands on the tablecloth or*
> *   your clothes.*

Henry VIII was a fastidious eater and did not require such advice (fig. 43). In any case, if he offended, few would have been prepared to risk his displeasure by pointing out his errors, especially towards the end of his reign.

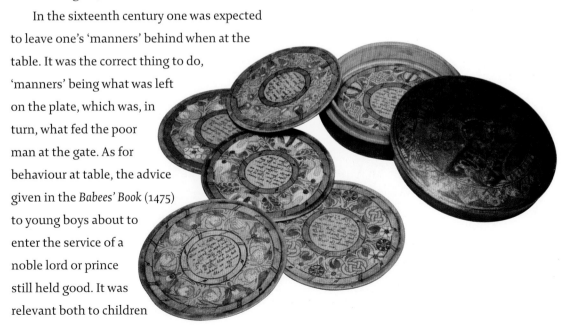

Jacobean Junketing

'A king's chaff is worth more than other men's corn.'

Seventeenth-century English proverb

46. Exotic fruits – as on this early seventeenth-century buffet painted by Georg Flegel – were not plentiful in Scotland. The nine-year-old James wrote to the Countess of Mar, thanking her for a present of fruit, a rare and special treat.

James I (1603–25) arrived in London on 11 May in the first year of his reign. His cold Scottish childhood had hardly been nourishing, with violence and murder before he was out of the womb; his father and mother respectively blown up and beheaded. In 1567, at the age of thirteen months, he had become King James VI of Scotland. He was kept in strict confinement in Stirling Castle, where, in his early years, he knew neither love nor companionship (fig. 47). His mind was shaped by an intense, spartan regime of academic studies, and as he grew he filled his heart with the few attractive young men who ventured to his court. This curious blend earned him early on the nickname from the French king Henri IV of the 'wisest fool in

Christendom'. It must have been something of a relief for James to come at last to England and, moreover, to be welcomed by the populace during his five-week journey south from Edinburgh to London, that rich city reputedly flowing with milk and honey (fig. 48).

James had not been raised with parental love, and he may also have been nutritionally starved. It is reported that he was unable to walk until he was five years old, and he suffered all his life from weak legs, a condition that his younger son also seems to have inherited, through either his genes or his diet.

An English gentleman, Fynes Moryson, wrote of his travels in Scotland in the last decade of the sixteenth century: 'They eat much

47. James VI of Scotland, attributed to Rowland Lockey, 1574. The young king, deprived of love, warmth and possibly even an adequate diet, is a sad figure.

48. Engraving by James Parker after Thomas Stothard, 1797. James VI of Scotland is pictured at the start of his new life as James I of England, although it would be another 100 years before a full union with Scotland was sanctioned.

red colewort and cabbage, but little fresh meate, using to salt their mutton and geese.' In a nobleman's house he was served 'great platters of porridge, each having a peece of sodden meate', and was surprised to see the servants sitting down to eat with the family. He did notice, however, that the family 'in steede of porridge had a pullet with some prunes and broth'. Oatcakes were commonly eaten, but he observed that, in towns, wheaten loaves were available for the gentry. All this is a far cry from Sir Walter Scott's romantic notions of the early Scottish diet with great joints of beef, haunches of venison and tables groaning with oven-hot hearty teatime fare. Given the genealogy of the Scottish royal family (James's maternal grandmother was French, and his mother was married to the king of France), some slight French influence may have made its way north of the border, although many of the ingredients necessary for the preparation of such dishes most probably did not.

Scotland was a poor and, in James's experience, violent country. He had taken to travelling its roads only when necessary, wearing a padded doublet against knife attacks. However, the English capital was not altogether the safe haven for which he had hoped. Before the first two years of his reign were out, the most serious attempt to bomb an English reigning monarch had been planned, and on his arrival in 1603 he found that the

49. In 1589 James I married Princess Anna of Denmark. She brought a little warmth into his life, and possibly also some of her native dishes: pork, rye bread, and pickled and salted fish. The diplomat Jacob Ulfeldt, seen here eating such food with his family in 1625, was chancellor to Anna's brother, Christian IV.

plague had beaten a path before him to the city's gates, causing the postponement of his coronation. He spent his first night in the city in the Tower of London, instead of the opulent Tudor apartments at Whitehall Palace, which was not a safe resort in time of plague. He then moved from the Tower to Greenwich and subsequently out of town altogether, first to Windsor and by Christmas to Hampton Court.

By this time James's Danish wife, Queen Anna, had joined him with two of their three children, Henry (aged nine) and Elizabeth (six); three-year-old Charles, a sickly child, was left a

while longer in Scotland. After the long reign of Elizabeth I, the Virgin Queen, it was seen as a great novelty to have a royal family. Christmas was James I's first period of festivity in England. He wrote invectives against the strict Scottish Kirk's bans on Sunday entertainment and Christmas celebrations, declaring that 'certaine days in the yeere should be appointed, for delighting the people ..., for convening of neighbours, for entertaining friendship and heartlinesse, by honest feasting and merrinesse'. Christmas, then, was to be a time for feasting, plays and masques.

The diplomat Dudley Carleton, who found himself in 'the fogs and mists' at Hampton Court during this Christmas of 1603, wrote to his friend John Chamberlain: 'We have had here a merry Christmas and nothing to disquiet us save brabbles amongst our ambassadors, and one or two poor companions that died of the plague.' The 'brabbling' ambassadors took it in turns to dine privately with the king for fear of arousing violent disagreements between them. What they dined on is unrecorded, but the main dish on the menu must surely have been the first performance of *Robin Goodfellow*, a play ill-suited perhaps for a Christmas festival, for we know it as *A Midsummer Night's Dream*. Acting in it, in the Great Hall at Hampton Court, was its author, William Shakespeare.

Also staged at Hampton Court was a Christmas masque. This art form developed under James I into a sumptuous entertainment, costing anything up to £2 million per performance in today's money. Masques were normally staged at Whitehall Palace, in the Banqueting House, which, contrary to its name, was not intended primarily for banqueting, but rather specifically designed for these

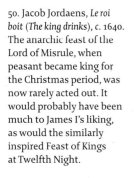

50. Jacob Jordaens, *Le roi boit (The king drinks)*, c. 1640. The anarchic feast of the Lord of Misrule, when peasant became king for the Christmas period, was now rarely acted out. It would probably have been much to James I's liking, as would the similarly inspired Feast of Kings at Twelfth Night.

51. Inigo Jones designed many of the lavish costumes for the masque participants. Queen Anna regularly took part in performances, in which she would dance but never speak.

52. James I and the Banqueting House by Paul van Somer, c. 1620. Early in his reign, James I built a banqueting house. When it burned down in 1619, he commissioned Inigo Jones to design the splendid building that still stands as the sole survival of the Palace of Whitehall.

performances (fig. 52). The most successful masques were written and designed by the dynamic duo of poet and playwright Ben Jonson and designer and architect Inigo Jones (fig. 51).

These spectacular performances were followed by a most extraordinary supper experience. One such, after the 'Masque of Blackness' at the Banqueting House in 1605, was described by Carleton in a letter: 'The night's work was concluded with a banquet in the great chamber, which was so seriously assaulted that down went tables and trestles before one bit [of food] was touched.' One would imagine this to have been an unfortunate but isolated incident, except that it recurred on Twelfth Night in 1618. The Venetian ambassador's chaplain, Orazio Busino, described the party that followed the masque:

> The King glanced round the table and departed and at once like so many harpies the company fell on their prey ... The repast was served on glass plates or dishes and at the first assault they upset the table; and the crash of glass platters reminded me precisely of a severe hailstorm at midsummer smashing the window glass. The story ended at half past two in the morning[,] and half disgusted and weary we returned home.

This may have been more than coincidence. Perhaps it was a Twelfth Night ritual. Carleton, writing from Venice in September 1613, seemed amazed that a banquet after a masque should ever take place *without* riot: 'The feast ended with a banquet – and all without disorder, which was strange in respect maskers were admitted to the dancing.' Another fashion in court suppers was to show the meal arranged on silver and gold plates on the buffet and then, before it was touched, to whisk it away, replacing it with an even more opulent supper.

Sometimes it was simply the amount of alcohol consumed without food before the show, during the long wait for the arrival of the royal family, that was the cause of culinary catastrophe, as during the visit of the queen's brother King Christian IV of Denmark in 1606. The courtier Sir John Harington reported that

> The lady who did play the Queen's part, did carry most precious gifts to both their majesties; but forgetting the steps arising to the canopy, overset her caskets into his Danish Majesty's lap, and fell at his feet, though I rather think it was in his face ... . His majesty then got up and would dance with the Queen of Sheba; but he fell down and humbled himself before her, and was carried to an inner chamber and laid on a bed of state; which was not a little defiled with the presents of the Queen bestowed on his garments; such as wine, cream, jelly, beverage, cakes, spices and other good matters. The entertainment and show went forward, and most of the presenters went backward, or fell down, wine did so occupy their

53. Banqueters in a lush interior by Hieronymus Janssens, seventeenth century. Over-consumption of alcohol may have been a factor in the disorder following the masque and the repeated demolition of the supper table.

inner chambers. *Now did appear, in rich dress, Hope, Faith and Charity. Hope did assay to speak, but wine rendered her efforts so feeble that she withdrew ... Faith was then all alone, for I am certain she was not joined with good works, and left the court in a staggering condition. Charity came to the King's feet, and seemed to cover the multitude of sins her sisters had committed; in some sort she made obeisance and brought*

gifts ... . She then returned to Hope and Faith, who were both sick and spewing in the lower hall ... . Victory ... after much lamentable utterance ... was led away like a silly captive, and laid to sleep on the outer steps of the antechamber. Now did Peace make entry ... and much contrary to her semblance, most rudely made war with her olive branch, and laid on the pates of those who did oppose her coming.

54. The poet Ben Jonson wrote a dedication to James I's drinking den in the undercroft of the Banqueting House: 'Since, Bacchus, thou art father/ Of wines, to thee the rather/ We dedicate this Cellar/ Where now thou art made dweller'.

eighteen, but surely this also represents the king's reflections on the very nature of kingship and his own performance as monarch. The observation that 'drunkenness ... is a beastlie vice, namely in a King: but specially beware with it, because it is one of those vices that increaseth with age' may well have been written from the heart, from his own personal experience.

James, although not inclined to public displays, was fond – perhaps over-fond – of the Scottish fraternity from which his court was largely composed. As the Puritan, anti-monarchist writer Lucy Hutchinson recalled, 'the court of this king was a nursery of lust and intemperance; he had brought in with him a company of hunger-starved poor Scots'. The fine Palladian Banqueting House that the king commissioned from Inigo Jones in 1619 contained an undercroft as a kind of drinking grotto for James and his friends, to be decorated with shellwork by Isaac de Caux (fig. 54).

An evening's drinking with the king in his cellar may well have required stiff fortification, according to a bigoted description the courtier Sir Anthony Weldon gave of the host: 'His eyes large, ever rolling after any stranger that came in his presence; his beard was very thin; his tongue too large for his mouth, which ever made him speak full in the mouth, and made him drink very uncomely, as if eating his drink, which came out in to the cup on

James I's own views on excessive drinking are set out clearly in the *Basilikon Doron, or His Majesty's Instructions to His Dearest Sonne, Henry the Prince* (1599), where he lists the four cardinal virtues as 'justice, prudence, temperance and fortitude [with] Temperance, queene of all the rest', adding: 'He cannot be thought worthy to rule and command others, that cannot rule and containe his own proper affections and unreasonable appetites.' Henry, his eldest son, unfortunately died at the tender age of

55. James I's counterblast to tobacco was published in 1672. James habitually went into print with his ideas, churning out pamphlets and books of advice to his son on how a king should govern.

each side of his mouth … His walk was ever circular, his fingers ever in that walk fiddling about his cod-piece.'

Private sessions in the king's drinking den have sadly, although perhaps fortunately, remained just that. But we do know from his physician, Sir Theodore de Mayerne, that the king's preference in wines inclined to sweetness above all: 'He promiscuously drinks beer, ale, Spanish wine, sweet French wine, white wine, Muscatel and sometimes Alicante wine. He does not care whether the wine be strong or not, so it is sweet.' James's personal tastes, then, were at variance with the Scots' general habit of drinking wine, which had so struck Fynes Moryson during his travels there in the 1590s: 'They drink pure wines, not with

sugar as the English, yet at feasts they put comfits in the wine, after the French manner.' However, one vice the king most surely did not possess was an addiction to the new fashionable weed – in his words the 'filthy', 'hurtfull', 'stinking suffumigation' – called tobacco (fig. 55).

At his first Christmas in England, James I was already aware of the difficulty of entertaining foreign ambassadors, who had to be treated with all the deference due to the kings they represented and who, in this context, considered the smallest gesture of the king as a token of respect or a mark of disdain for their royal masters. One of the king's first acts, therefore, was to appoint a Master of Ceremonies to provide a dignified welcome to a new ambassador, find him and his retinue appropriate lodgings, organize his travel and orchestrate the detailed protocol required for his audience with the king. The underlying agenda was to show hospitality and maintain good relations with foreign nations, while keeping costs down as far as possible and smoothing over the ambassador's tantrums when he felt his status was being compromised in any way (fig. 56). The rivalry between ambassadors for royal honours became literally cut-throat. Sulking and 'brabbling' could in an instant turn into fighting between the liveried servants of two hostile nations, in the manner of warring camps of football fans. Dudley

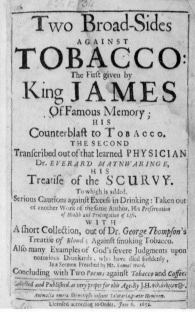

end of the board, above his majesty. There was [*sic*] six cart-loads of plate, brought from the Tower, at this banquet, wherewith two stately stages were furnished, one very large and spacious, valued at £200,000; and the other far less, but valued at £500,000. All was sent back to the Tower the next day.' On another occasion, the Duke of Buckingham hosted a dinner for the king, the prince and the Spanish ambassadors at York House, 'where it is said', reported a correspondent of Mead, that 'there were 3000 dishes of meat' (fig. 57).

Queen Elizabeth I had chosen never to dine in public, although she went through the motions of having the food laid out in a state room in the royal manner. Her ladies would

56. James I dining with the Spanish ambassador, c. 1624. An ambassador represented his sovereign and expected to be treated with every mark of deference at meals and entertainments.

57. The Duke of Buckingham, the favourite of James I and friend of Charles I, gave the most elaborate dinners, often to the royal family, at his house off the Strand. Food might appear from clouds like ambrosial manna. He never failed to surprise.

Carleton wrote that the Florentine and Spanish ambassadors could not meet without blood being shed.

The Spanish ambassador, the Count of Gondomar, with his entourage of 220, was on one occasion lodged in the queen's own residence, Somerset House, and was feasted at the Banqueting House in Whitehall, 'furnished as if it were for the king his master[,] and great care is taken that no curiosities for diet shall be wanting' (as reported by Carleton). According to the Revd Joseph Mead of Cambridge, at this feast 'sugar-works represented a complete army of horse and foot, with drums, ensigns &c. They say he [Gondomar] was placed at the

58. A well-stocked kitchen of the early seventeenth century. The great variety of food served to the court would cater for any taste.

then retrieve the dishes and carry them to an inner chamber, where she could eat in private. James I had initially been enraptured by the public's enthusiasm for him, and dined in public regularly. After the Gunpowder Plot of 1605, however, he became more wary, living and dining (the Venetian ambassador noted) in his 'innermost rooms with only Scotsmen about him'. On one occasion, when he was urged to show himself more to his people, he angrily retorted: 'God's wounds! I will pull down my breeches and they shall also see my arse!'

The king was fed on a diet based on meat, strongly featuring venison and game, often made into pies. A meal served to him at Houghton Hall in Norfolk in 1617 included capon, duck, veal, mutton, venison, swan, turkey, goose and pork with venison, chicken and tripe pies, with extra plates of wild boar and sliced beef humble pie for supper. Hot pheasant and six quails are mentioned in the menu as special dishes for the king.

Sir Walter Scott's revelation that James I's favourite food was atholl brose – porridge with whisky and honey – has a romantic ring, but lacks any evidence. We do know that when his beloved Duke of Buckingham was ill, the king sent him gifts of cherries, melons, pears, strawberries and raspberries, perhaps recalling his own childhood delight in being sent gifts of fresh fruit. Although he claimed that a meal of red deer and garlic pie, with a tobacco pipe to follow, was fit only for the Devil, he sent Buckingham as a tonic 'the eyes, the tongue and the dowsets [testicles]' of a deer he had killed, and his favourite remedy for the gout was to put his hands into the belly and bathe his bare feet and legs in the warm blood of a newly killed stag. Buckingham administered his own remedies to the king as he lay ill with a 'tertian ague' (fever) at Royston, Hertfordshire, in the spring of 1625. When the king died on 27 March, the usual cries of 'Poison!' filled the air, but in this case they were almost certainly ill-founded.

'More strait and private than in former times', although observing ceremony with order and decorum, was the first description (by John Chamberlain) of the court of the new king, Charles I (1625–49). Carvers, cupbearers and waiters would be standing by from ten in the morning, ready to serve the king's dinner with court ceremony and on bended knee, as he called for it.

In June Charles went to welcome to England his French bride, Henrietta Maria, in Dover, where they shared their first meal. The king, with his own hands, served her carved pheasant and venison, and she ate with a good appetite, despite whispered warnings from her confessor, constantly at her elbow,

59. Sir Anthony van Dyck, *Charles I and Henrietta Maria*, c. 1630. Their marriage was stormy until the king's favourite, the Duke of Buckingham, was assassinated; the queen's French retinue was sent home, and Henrietta Maria was soon pregnant with the son and heir, the future Charles II.

60. Hunting at Nonsuch
Palace, Surrey, in the early
seventeenth century.
Red deer pie, presumably
cooked without garlic,
was a popular item on
the king's menu. James I
was passionately fond
of hunting, and spent as
much time as possible in
his hunting lodges.

that it was a Church fast day. Following the wedding breakfast at Whitehall, the Duke of Buckingham entertained the royal couple with a great show of magnificence, serving up among other delicacies a 6-foot sturgeon, which, it was said, had leapt into a sculler's boat from the River Thames.

The practice of dining in public and the plethora of clergymen around the dining table soon caused friction for the young royal couple. A courtier at the public dining ceremony gave his impression of Henrietta Maria: 'The Queen, howsoever very little of stature, is yet of a pleasing countenance, if she be pleased, but full of spirit and vigour, and seems of a more than ordinary resolution. With one frown, diverse of us being at Whitehall to see her, being at dinner … she drove us all out of the chamber. I suppose none but a Queen could have cast such a scowl.'

Then there was the question of whether Roman Catholic or Church of England grace should be said at the royal table. Joseph Mead reported that

the King and Queen dining together in the presence, Mr Hacket … being there to say grace, the confessor would have prevented him, but that Hacket shoved him away; whereupon the confessor went to the Queen's side, and was about to say grace again, but that the king pulling the dishes unto him, and the carvers falling to their

61. Detail from *Charles I,
Queen Henrietta Maria, and
Charles, Prince of Wales,
Dining in Public* by Gerrit
Houckgeest, 1635 (see
fig. 69 for the whole
painting). The practice
of dining every day in
the public gaze and the
antagonism between
the queen's Catholic and
the king's Protestant
clergymen over the grace
caused daily friction for
the royal couple.

*business, hindered. When dinner was done …
Mr Hacket again got the start. The confessor,
nevertheless, begins his grace as loud as
Mr Hacket, with such a confusion, that the king
in great passion instantly rose from the table,
and, taking the queen by the hand, retired into
the bedchamber.*

On his accession to the throne, Charles I
appointed an extremely able Master of
Ceremonies, Sir John Finet, whose notebooks
give us an insight into the problems he
encountered in his work and the way he dealt
with them. In the previous reign, the Cofferer
of the royal household had had to settle all
expenses of ambassadors and their retinues,
such as food, coal, light, beer, wine and bread.
Charles sought to end this practice and to base
hospitality on what was being offered to the
ambassadors' English counterparts overseas.
They were now asked to bring their own cooks,
plate and even table linen, although this last
seems to have been provided where required.
A new problem arose: the ambassadors began
regularly to refuse what was on offer as being
too little to satisfy their honour, and to make
their own excessive demands. Fortunately
Finet was adept at dealing with these childish
outbursts. When the dukes of Württemberg
and Saxony asked to be invited to the king's
birthday dinner at Somerset House, the
queen replied in frustration that 'she should

be less happy than any common country
gentlewoman if she would not make one meal
in a year without the presence of unknown
faces'. This unhappy news had to be relayed
to the dukes by Finet, although he had a
sweetener to offer them in the form of an
invitation to the play following the dinner.
They petulantly refused, however, saying that
if they were not wanted at the dinner, they
could not be wanted at the play. Finet could not
allow them to return home unappeased, and
eventually persuaded them into accompanying
the king and queen to a specially arranged
second viewing of the play, where they were
shown every attention, as Finet summed up,
'with some reparations of former omissions'.

Placed between the king and the
ambassador, Finet often bore the brunt of
both parties' antagonism towards each other.
The king expected rich pickings from the City
of London to pay for ambassadors' visits, and
was not slow to requisition houses for their
accommodation. Refusal could result in a
prison sentence for the householder.
Sometimes the ambassadors could simply
misunderstand the protocol, as when the
Venetian ambassador made his own way to
London and had to sneak back to Greenwich
'wythout noyse' to be met there by the king's
barge in the proper manner.

Charles battled with the conflicting needs
to have his royal household functioning in a

62. The Banqueting House at Whitehall Palace was the most prestigious venue in which to stage the initial visit of a foreign ambassador. Charles I commissioned Sir Peter Paul Rubens to paint ceiling canvases depicting the Stuart dynasty. Here, James I is depicted as Solomon, the wise ruler.

63. Sir Anthony van Dyck, *Queen Henrietta Maria with Sir Jeffrey Hudson*, 1633. The queen called her 18-inch-tall human 'pet' Lord Minimus, and dressed him in fashionable clothes. At the age of thirty he was captured by Barbary pirates, and during his stay with them, he grew, unaccountably, to almost 4 feet in height.

manner becoming to the kingly state and to cut his expenditure. At the end of his first year on the throne, he attempted to limit the tables at his court to five including his own. No money was forthcoming in lieu of victuals for those used to eating at the king's expense, however, and within a couple of weeks the tables were reinstated. The Duke of Buckingham, that great showman of the age, had no such inhibitions. He spent wildly, endlessly producing sumptuous banquets for James I and later Charles at his residence, York House. Many dinners included elaborate entertainment; some were estimated to have cost the duke over £5000. There were pies containing live frogs, which hopped on to the table, or birds that flew out into the air. His most successful piece of banqueting theatre has to be the presentation of a large pie, out of which leapt a seven-year-old boy only 18 inches high, dressed as a knight. He was Jeffrey Hudson, and he was a present for Henrietta Maria (fig. 63). The queen lavished care on him, dressing him in fancy clothes, as she might a doll. Nevertheless, Hudson had an eventful life, often being carried around at court in the pocket of the giant Welsh porter, William Evans, and at one stage being kidnapped by Barbary pirates, causing 'more upset at court', according to an unnamed courtier, 'than if they had lost a fleet'.

Although the king was naturally abstemious in both food and drink, he was

still served twenty-eight dishes at a sitting. Even a courtier might expect sixteen dishes on his table, together with bread, beer and wine.

The image of divine kingship, so clearly expressed in Rubens's paintings on the ceiling of the Banqueting House (fig. 62), was provoking hostility in the country. In 1642, as the money drained from the royal coffers and Parliamentary forces gathered, king and court left London for Oxford, and the country sank into civil war. Even after the king fell into the

64. The fleeting days of plenty, depicted here in a detail from *Taste, Hearing and Touch* by Jan Brueghel the Elder (*c.* 1620), were drawing to an end, as king and parliament prepared for conflict. Almost to the end of his life, Charles I dined in public, in accordance with the rites of his God-given heritage.

65. Herrings were always a good, cheap source of protein and, salted in barrels, would help to keep Oliver Cromwell's model army in tiptop condition through the winter months.

66. A contemporary political cartoon showing Charles I imprisoned in Carisbrooke Castle, Isle of Wight, *c.* 1648. So much effort had been put into planning the king's escape that it seemed almost certain to succeed. If Mrs Hammond had not been such a good cook, English history might have been rather different.

and supper, once of Beer, and once of Wine and Water mixt, only after Fish a glass of French wine; the Beverage he himself mix'd at the Cupboard, so he would have it. He very seldom ate and drank before Dinner, nor between Meals.' Later at Newmarket, Herbert relates that 'the Presence chamber was constantly thronged with people, especially when His Majesty was at dinner or supper, and he seldom or never failed to dine in publick'.

After escaping from Hampton Court Palace in November 1647, Charles spent a year under the care of Governor Robert Hammond at Carisbrooke Castle on the Isle of Wight, a place of refuge that became a prison (fig. 66). The situation was unprecedented, and nobody quite knew how to behave. Hammond was a gourmet, and thought he could at least feed the king well. He sent to Chertsey for his mother to come and help with the cooking. Dinner continued with its twenty-eight dishes, although by March 1648 this had been reduced

hands of the Parliamentarians in early 1647, the ritual of royal dining continued. It was noted by the historian Sir Thomas Herbert that at Holdenby House near Northampton, where Charles was kept for a short while in 1647, his dinner was signalled by the sound of trumpets, and he was served as at court, 'eating but of few dishes, and, as he used to say, agreeable to his exercise, drinking but twice every dinner

67. Charles I was executed on 30 January 1649. A witness remarked: 'There was such a groan by the thousands then present as I never heard before and desire I may never hear again.'

to sixteen. Even so, the royal guest, with no more exercise than a walk on the castle battlements or a game of bowls, and no other amusements, came to relish the home cooking provided with such care by Mrs Hammond.

Charles had retained a core of servants, who also had to adapt to the situation. As the king spent most of his time alone, it was primarily at dinner that he socialized, asking for news of events in the country and talking about theology with Hammond's young chaplain. He also took the opportunity to relay messages to his Clerk of the Kitchen, Abraham Dowcett, regarding the letters he was smuggling from his prison via Mrs Wheeler, his laundress. They evolved a series of secret signs. The king would signal that he had a letter in his bedchamber ready to be taken to Mrs Wheeler for dispatch, and news of the progress of these letters was relayed by Dowcett: a dropped handkerchief meaning the letter had been dispatched the previous Monday, or a dropped glove meaning that it had gone since. When the packet had been delivered, Dowcett would talk of a delivery of asparagus, and when it looked certain that it would be, he would speak to the king of artichokes. The king's Gentleman Usher,

Osborne, used the interaction at dinner to slip notes into the fingers of the king's gloves, while his Page of the Bedchamber, Henry Firebrace, hatched a plan for escape. The scheme was carefully thought through and diligently prepared. Rope was smuggled into the king's bedchamber, fast horses were waiting outside the castle walls, and a boat was harboured to take him off the island instantly to France. All went to plan; it was a moonless night and the guards were getting noisily drunk. There was one sticking point – and that was the king. Because of Hammond's groaning gourmet tables, Charles, for the first time in his life, had put on weight and could no longer squeeze as rehearsed through the bars of his window. In fact, he became wedged, and only with difficulty could he get back into his room, where he instantly lit a candle to signal that the escape had been aborted. The king's new appetite had been his undoing, and possibly changed the course of British history.

Just before 1 pm on 30 January 1649, at Whitehall Palace, Charles I ate his final meal, a piece of bread and half a glass of claret, before walking on to the scaffold to his execution (fig. 67). The courtier William Herbert wrote that it was 'the saddest sight England ever saw'.

Restoration Ritual and Sexy Snacks

'For what preserves you King more than ceremony? ...
You cannot put upon you too much King.'

Duke of Newcastle to Charles II, 1642

68. Charles II by Rosalind Thornycroft, 1932. The king provided a popular spectacle with daily public dining, but in the evening he could relax with friends or one of his mistresses.

The five-year-old Charles, Prince of Wales (later Charles II, 1660–85) dines in state with his parents at Whitehall Palace. He sits at the end of the table, to the left of his mother, Queen Henrietta Maria, who sits at the left hand of the king, Charles I. The young prince already has his own silver-gilt vessels, made by the Jewel House. Sewers, or servers, on bended knee offer dishes to the king and his family. The prince chooses from the food offered, and the gentlemen carve and taste each portion before it is placed before him. A procession of liveried servants carry in more dishes and lay them on the table, where none but the royal family dines. Over the king's head is the canopy of state, erected for him alone. Behind a balustrade at the end of the chamber, well-dressed courtiers and men (mainly men) of quality press to witness every mouthful of the royal meal. As if to counteract all this formality, a clutch of dogs play and probably defecate around the table. This is the formative experience of having dinner for Charles I's eldest son, who, after years of struggle, heartbreak and exile, will return to England to re-create almost exactly this ritual of royal public dining. In between he will know danger, hunger and despair, but also loyalty, comradeship and love. He will remember that bread and cheese are better than an empty stomach, but he will never forget that he is the rightful heir to the English and Scottish thrones.

69. Gerrit Houckgeest, *Charles I, Queen Henrietta Maria, and Charles, Prince of Wales, Dining in Public*, 1635 (see also detail, fig. 61). Royal dining in public changed very little over the years. Some sovereigns enjoyed the ritual, others loathed it. It was not until the reign of George III that it finally died out.

Prince Charles's first food in this world had come not from his mother, Henrietta Maria, but from Mrs Christabella Wyndham, his wet nurse, who (rumour has it) was also his first lover, fifteen years later. The infant prince almost immediately had his own household, which included a private or privy kitchen. How much say he had in his diet, as he grew older, is unrecorded. He was a large, dark, robust child who was rarely sick, but on one occasion during a fever, his physician fed him chicken broth laced with senna and rhubarb. It seems to have done the trick and restored him to full health.

From 1641, national events – and the diet of Charles, who was then eleven – took a turn for the worse. His visit that year to Cambridge to see the Ferrars family, where he ate a humble meal of apple pie and cheese, was a taste of things to come. The final royal feast of his father's reign, on the marriage of his nine-year-old sister, Mary, to Prince William of Orange, was, unusually, a private family meal.

During the Civil War, as we have seen, Charles I and his court moved to Oxford, where they attempted to maintain the rituals of court life. The king dined in public, while the Prince of Wales, in a rally for royal support, was feasted by the Welsh in feudal fashion at Raglan Castle in Monmouthshire, on fat goat, eaten off gold plate. However, it soon became apparent that the cause was all but lost. Charles bade his father a fond farewell and fled to the West Country, where his desperate condition was slightly alleviated by a somewhat softer cuisine of cherry pie and clotted cream.

By 1646, the Prince of Wales had been forced from the mainland and was in exile in Jersey. Freed from the most pressing concern of being captured by Parliamentarian troops, he set up his own court at Elizabeth Castle in St Helier, where he dined in public, as at Whitehall. This was not just a parade of empty plates; local butchers, farmers and fishermen were obliged to reserve their produce for the prince at the local market until noon every Wednesday. Daily requirements for the fledgling court and its numerous retainers could be in the order of two or three sheep and lambs, veal, pork, a couple of chickens and geese, as well as two pots of butter and two dozen eggs. The prince now sat alone at his table, wearing his hat, after his chaplain had said grace and his carver, taster and cupbearer had performed their offices on bended knee, following the rinsing of the royal fingers in a silver-gilt bowl. The royalist population of the island flocked to see the new attraction – one observer reported that it was 'a delight to behold' – despite the financial hardship it must have cost many of them.

Within a few months, the curtain came down on this little interlude of royal theatre as the real-life drama of the king approached its tragic denouement and the Prince of Wales set off for the safer shores of France. There,

70. This charming portrait of Charles II as Prince of Wales was painted for his mother by Sir Anthony van Dyck in 1637 or early 1638. Little did anyone think at the time that armour was to be necessary to his young life, not just as a romantic costume for a portrait but also for his very survival.

71. While England was in the grip of Puritanism, the 'gloire' of royal French building, art and cuisine was going from strength to strength under the young and dynamic Louis XIV. This supper pavilion was prepared for the fetes at Versailles in 1668.

however, he no longer ruled a little fiefdom of his own, but was obliged to defer to his mother, Henrietta Maria, now established there, and to beg his bread from his cousin, the child-king Louis XIV, in a country ruled by the Regent Queen Mother and Cardinal Mazarin. Having relished the taste of his own table, Charles was not slow in escaping to The Hague in The Netherlands, where he lived for a while with his sister Mary and her husband, the Prince of Orange. As the Prince of Wales, Charles dined at a table with his sister; his brother-in-law ate at a separate table, at which he was frequently joined by the country's statesmen, whom protocol would have forbidden to be invited to the English royal table.

In early February 1649, Charles's chaplain entered his presence, addressing him with the dreaded words 'Your Majesty'. King Charles I had been beheaded by his own subjects at Whitehall on 30 January. Now the king in exile, Charles was seated next to Louis XIV on a chair of state when he dined with him in what the memoir writer Françoise Bertaut de Motteville described as 'a truly royal dinner'. Having become slightly more eligible marriage material, he was courted by, among others, Anne Marie Louise d'Orléans, Duchess of Montpensier, who, however, lost interest during a grand dinner when the prospective bridegroom's table manners disgraced him in her eyes. Faced with a dish of ortolans – a small bird, renowned as the greatest of all French delicacies (fig. 72) – Charles turned up his nose in favour of a plate of good old English roast beef.

Following a disorganized sally into Scotland, Charles II's first coronation took place on 1 January 1651 in the ancient abbey of Scone in Perthshire. The coronation dinner consisted of partridges, calves' heads and twenty-two salmon; on the tables were damask napkins hastily embroidered with the king's new monogram, CR. England, however, was

not ready for the new king, and his foray southwards ended in failure – but not without a few culinary adventures along the way. After the decisive Battle of Worcester in September, Charles was forced into hiding. Kitted out in green breeches, a coarse shirt and doeskin doublet, an old greasy crowned hat and patched stockings with shoes that had to be altered to fit but still gave him blisters, he must have cut a remarkable figure as he limped, with his billhook, along country tracks in his assumed job of mending hedges. His protectors, the Penderels, a family of yeomen farmers at Boscobel House in Shropshire, risked their lives shopping for wine and biscuits for him in Wolverhampton, as by this time there was a £1000 ransom on the king's head and suspicions were easily aroused. Charles's diet during these September days consisted mainly of bread, cheese and beer with milk and eggs as a treat. After his night hiding in the famous oak tree, the king was starving (fig. 73). What I would not give for a roast mutton dinner, he must have told the heroic Penderel, who, having no mutton in the larder, set off to slaughter one of his neighbour's sheep. He would regale listeners for the rest of his life with the tale of how he and the king of England had roasted collops of mutton leg over the fire while the country searched high and low for the royal fugitive (and the neighbour for the lost sheep).

73. This silk tapestry, made c. 1665, commemorates Charles II's famous night hiding in the oak tree. The story caught the public imagination, and Royal Oak Day was long celebrated on 29 May, Charles II's birthday and the date of his Restoration.

Curiously, immediately following this episode, it was Charles's lack of culinary expertise that almost led to his downfall. In his disguise as a servant on his way back to France, he was asked by the cook of an inn to wind up the smoke jack – a task totally beyond his experience. His ineptitude, he was forced to explain, was a result of the newness of his situation and his impoverished upbringing.

Back in France, Queen Henrietta Maria insisted that her son eat at her table with his brother, the Duke of York, and his sister Princess Henrietta Anne. In addition to the humiliation of again being robbed of his status, he also had now, at his mother's demand, somehow to find funds to pay his expenses. Lord Rochester was sent as an ambassador to the Holy Roman Emperor to plead for a pension for his master, but the little money he managed to obtain he spent on a fine homecoming present for the king, of Christmas plum porridge, mince pies, cooked meats and brawn. If the food of the exile is hope, Charles certainly had little enough of that to live on at this stage.

Penniless and depressed, the wandering king left France with a small pension. Being refused entry to Holland, he decamped to Spa, where his widowed sister Mary joined him for the summer months of 1653. In the autumn they went to Cologne, where the king was settled enough to establish a skeleton household with two cooks, a baker and a sommelier. The exiled king was nevertheless still living in some degree of deprivation and certainly debt; given a pack of hounds, he declared he could not afford to feed them, but at least he did not roast them on the spit. Yet, from surviving accounts, it would appear that the king's cooks, John Sayers and Giles Rose, fed the peripatetic royal person and court rather well. Dinner on 5 November 1655 consisted of roast chicken, partridge, veal, stewed quinces and fresh fruit, followed by a supper of roast mutton with gravy, pigeon, lark and crayfish, with stewed apples and fresh fruit for dessert. For breakfast, still not a universal meal, the king ate eggs, bacon and sausages,

74. Jan Baptiste van
Meunincxhove, *Charles II
and His Brothers Dining in
Bruges in the Late 1650s*,
seventeenth century. The
king dines in public and is
served in royal style. On the
table is an impressive salt,
similar in design to those
he commissioned on his
return to England.

75. Le Pâtissier, seventeenth century. Marie de' Medici had introduced delicate sweet pastries to France from Italy during the first half of the seventeenth century. French pastries became – and remained – very popular and were of superb quality, frequently figuring in menus for Charles II.

76. Eleven silver-gilt salts of this type were made in England for Charles II in 1661. They are known as St George's Salts and were for use at banquets. They are now kept in the Jewel House at the Tower of London.

great salt, silver-gilt plates, spoons, forks and four gold dinner plates, which he set on tablecloths embroidered with his monogram beneath a royal crown. These were the basic items required for the royal performance; for the rest, hired pewter plates could make up the numbers required. The star of the show made sure that he used all the remaining props in his box to play his God-given role. He appeared at table resplendent in the blue sash of the Order of the Garter, with its glittering diamond star pinned to his coat and the garter itself tied fetchingly around his well-proportioned leg.

But deliverance was at hand. After the death of Oliver Cromwell on 3 September 1658,

or, if he preferred, eggs beaten up with sugar and lemons. There were always 'extraordinary' celebration suppers for the king's birthday on 29 May, and his Christmas dinner in 1655 was roast beef, collar of boar and chicken with plum pudding, followed by fruit tart, plum broth and mince pies, costing twice the normal daily budget of 21 guilders.

Charles was hardly scraping the barrel; nor was the service itself lacking. He might be minus a crown and a country, but wherever he went he was determined to appear every inch a king (fig. 74). The ceremony at his table, wherever he found himself, followed as strictly as possible the ritual he had known as a child at Whitehall. He had by this stage acquired a

77. Charles II dines at the Mauritshuis in The Hague in 1660, just before his return to England. He is seated under a canopy of state with his immediate family around him. His Dutch hosts sit at the adjoining table.

made Master of the Horse, and others faithful in exile were also rewarded with important positions. James Butler, Earl of Ormonde was created a duke and made Lord Steward of the King's Household, and Charles's faithful cook John Sayers grew rich and fat in the kitchen, introducing members of his family into lucrative household situations. The king restored the Presence Chamber as a room in which he could dine in public. He also reorganized the royal bedchamber in the French style, with the bed in a railed-off alcove, to double as a room for levées, the king's morning rising ceremony, at which he would receive invited guests.

his son Richard, derisively known as 'Tumbledown Dick', was quite clearly not up to the job of running the country. After thirteen years in exile, Charles was finally invited home, and it was hardly a moment too soon (fig. 77). By this time the king was thin and irritable, and had even been forced to sell his plate and eat his meals from a simple trencher. He arrived in London to cheering crowds on 29 May 1660, his thirtieth birthday.

Despite the civil wars, the Whitehall Palace to which Charles II returned was much as he had known it as a child, and he immediately set about forming his household there. General George Monck, who had engineered the king's return, was created Duke of Albemarle and

The king must have had an overriding desire to please his new, enthusiastic subjects, those retainers who had loyally supported him during the long years of exile, and – not least – at last himself. Pleasing, however, usually comes at a cost, which someone has to bear. Well-disposed and accessible as he was as king, Charles II needed increasingly to tax his people to raise the revenue for his generosity and the hospitality of his court, which was certainly producing the desired effect, as was recorded early in his reign by Edward Chamberlayne: 'The magnificence and abundant plenty of our King's Tables, hath caused amazement in Foreigners ... and the Natives, who were there freely welcome, to increase their affection to the King ... the English, who ever delighted in Feasting'.

78. To celebrate his restoration, the City of Exeter presented Charles II with a silver-gilt salt of state in the shape of a castle and studded with precious gems; see fig. 157. Plymouth gave him this most elegant silver-gilt table fountain, crowned with figures of Poseidon, god of the sea, and nymphs.

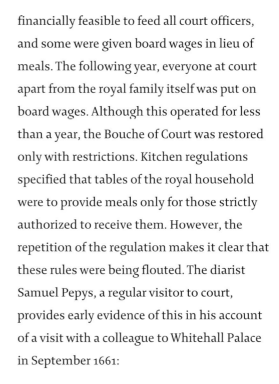

In return for a grant from Parliament, the king gave up the right to requisition provisions at an agreed discounted price for the use of the crown. This method, called purveyance, had often been a bone of contention, but it had kept the royal household supplied at below-market prices. The only alternative was to negotiate contract prices with suppliers, and so, inevitably, prices rose. As early as 1662 it was no longer

financially feasible to feed all court officers, and some were given board wages in lieu of meals. The following year, everyone at court apart from the royal family itself was put on board wages. Although this operated for less than a year, the Bouche of Court was restored only with restrictions. Kitchen regulations specified that tables of the royal household were to provide meals only for those strictly authorized to receive them. However, the repetition of the regulation makes it clear that these rules were being flouted. The diarist Samuel Pepys, a regular visitor to court, provides early evidence of this in his account of a visit with a colleague to Whitehall Palace in September 1661:

> To Mr Sayres, the Master Cook, and there we had a good slice of beef or two to our breakfast, and from thence he took us into the wine cellar where, by my troth, we were very merry, and I drank too much wine, and all along had great and particular kindness from Mr Sayres, but I drank so much wine that I was not fit for business, and therefore at noon I went and walked in Westminster Hall a while, and thence to Salisbury Court play house, where was acted the first time 'Tis Pity She's a Whore' …

In effect, every Tom, Dick and Samuel was being provided with free victuals at the cook's whim and the king's expense.

79. A blue-and-white tin-glazed earthenware plate made in The Netherlands, c. 1662, depicting Charles II and Queen Catherine soon after their marriage.

Barely affected in the long term, however, was the king's own table, at which, to the accompaniment of a small group of string players, he dined in public almost daily. Regardless of whether the king was there or not, the newly reintroduced 'Board of State' dictated that the royal dinner should be served mid-afternoon in the Presence Chamber.

For particularly grand occasions, when the king entertained foreign dignitaries or held the annual dinner for the Knights of the Garter, he made use of Inigo Jones's magnificent Banqueting House with its ceiling painted by

Rubens. There, as in the Presence Chamber, the king sat at a separate table under the canopy of state – a permanent fixture in both Presence Chamber and Banqueting House. However, as there was no designated dining room at court, tables were brought in as required. The object of all this trouble and expense was not primarily the king's meal; he could eat anywhere. It was rather to show the king in his regal splendour, seated at a table of plenty. For this to be fully achieved, an audience was required, vetted to complete the illusion of grandeur. According to the household ordinances, ushers allowed in only 'persons of good fashion and good appearance that have a desire to see us at dinner', while keeping out their servants, those of mean appearance and any other riff-raff. The demand for a glimpse of the masticating royal mouth was unquenchable. The swarm of spectators was confined behind a balustrade or rail in all the palaces where the king dined, and the valuable plate on the buffet kept out of their rapacious reach. It all smacks somewhat distastefully of the chimpanzees' tea parties staged in the 1950s. Yet, there lingered also an air of holy ritual, with the table as an altar, the sewers as altar boys and the carver, cupbearer and taster as priests.

Whatever the watching crowds had come to see, they were not always containable, and there were incidents where the barrier gave way, causing upset or injury. Sometimes people

80. Wenceslaus Hollar, *Garter Banquet in St George's Hall*, 1671. According to John Evelyn, 'the king sat on an elevated throne at a table alone and was served by the lords and pensioners'. During the dinner, 'the banqueting stuff was flung about the room profusely'.

scrambled at the end of the meal for whatever fruit or sweetmeats might be left on the table. At a dinner given by the Grand Duke of Tuscany in May 1669 for the king and the Duke of York, according to the account of Cosimo de' Medici's travels by Count Lorenzo Magalotti, the final course of fruit was plundered even before the diners had tasted it 'by the people who came to see the spectacle of the entertainment'. For the sake of dining in royal splendour, all this had to be endured (fig. 80).

If royal dinner was a matter of duty, supper was a different kettle of fish. Here the king could please himself. He often supped out with old and new friends of the nobility, or entertained 'the merry gang', the wits of the court; although more often than not he would be found supping privately with his current mistress. Both Barbara Castlemaine, Duchess of Cleveland and Louise de Kérouaille, Duchess of Portsmouth were given Whitehall apartments more lavish than those occupied by the queen. Nell Gwyn had a house in Pall Mall, next to St James's Palace, where she frequently entertained the king (fig. 81). Mutton and beer feature largely in her household bills, but so do larks, salmon, blue figs and lemon tart, presumably for intimate royal suppers. The bills for 'chane [China] oringes, greate pares, pertatus', 'sinomon' and much else besides were picked up by the Treasury. Kind-hearted Nell left in her will a sum for mutton and beer for the six men who would ring the bells at St Martin-in-the-Fields in her memory every Thursday evening.

Towards the end of Charles II's life, the Italian beauty Hortense Mancini, Duchess of Mazarin joined the sisterhood. She frequently

81. Nell Gwyn by Simon Verelst, *c. 1670*. 'Odd's fish, what company am I got into?!' exclaimed Gwyn when the king and his brother took her out for a drink in a tavern, only to discover that they had no money. Charles II's most popular mistress described herself as 'the Protestant whore'.

entertained the infatuated king at her home in Chelsea, where her friend Charles de Saint-Evremond superintended suppers of fine French cuisine and sparkling champagne. The diarist John Evelyn described the king's relationships with such women at court as 'luxurious dallying and profaneness', and the ladies themselves as the 'pleasure and curse of our nation'.

Amid the jollity of the king, his mistresses and their clutch of children, several of whom were also accommodated at Whitehall, moved the solitary figure of the queen, Catherine of Braganza, whom Charles had married in 1662. It was perhaps symptomatic of her life in England that on her arrival at Portsmouth, when she asked for a cup of tea, she was promptly handed a glass of ale. She was not slow in discovering the king's bevy of mistresses at court and their progeny, and it was perhaps the misfortune that she bore no children that exacerbated both her lack of status and the tensions of her relationship with the king. The queen was abstemious in both food and drink, and for the early part of the reign relied on the Portuguese cooks who had arrived with her to make her favourite bouillons. In a cupboard in her bedchamber she kept a supply of oranges, lemons, ginger, sugar, saffron and barley, probably to make drinks. A custom that she was successful in introducing into court was the drinking of tea, a pleasant social habit with which Catherine had been familiar in Portugal since her childhood.

Tea was not entirely unknown in England, but coffee, another relatively new drink, had so far proved more popular. Coffee was drunk almost exclusively in the coffee houses, the first of which had opened in Oxford in 1651, and those in London from 1652 (fig. 83). Charles II, momentarily concerned about seditious talk going on behind their doors, made a feeble attempt to outlaw the 250 coffee houses in London in December 1675, but public protest made sure that the ban was almost instantly withdrawn. Tea was also drunk in these

establishments, as well as chocolate, sherbet and alcoholic drinks, but coffee took precedence. Catherine's idea of tea-drinking, by contrast, came from a very different culture: it was drunk at home and in the main by women with their friends (fig. 82).

From the 1670s, tea slowly gained popularity in fashionable English circles. Imported from China and very expensive to buy, it was stored in a tin or box to keep it cool, and locked for safety. Pepys records in June 1667 his 'wife making of tea, a drink which Mr Pelling, the apothecary, tells her is good for her cold and defluxions'. This was obviously

83. A London coffee house, 1668. The coffee houses clustered around St James's and the City were considered to be rather racy, attracting a strictly male clientele. They developed into the London clubs, a place for men to smoke and discuss news and politics.

84. Hendrick Danckerts, *Charles II Being Presented with a Pineapple by the Royal Gardener John Rose*, 1675. It was impossible to grow pineapples in England, and long sea journeys meant that the fruit was often rotten when it arrived. It was a rare specimen indeed that landed, wholesome and fragrant, on the royal plate.

a new drink for an upwardly mobile family, and one perceived to be beneficial to health. Leading wits at Charles's court in exile in France had already discovered the health-giving properties of 'this great remedy' (as one broadsheet called it), which was claimed to be a cure or palliative for just about anything. However, tea would have to wait until the eighteenth century to take off properly at court, and then for prices to drop after the creation

of plantations in India, to establish itself as England's favourite beverage.

If tea was considered unusual in the seventeenth century, the pineapple must have been the pinnacle of exoticism (fig. 84). James I had received a pineapple forty years earlier, but it was in August 1661 that John Evelyn records his first sighting of a 'Queen Pine brought from Barbadoes and presented to his Majesty', although he remembers that Cromwell had

Right: 85. This engraving from 1683 shows the operation for the removal of a bladder stone. 'The stone', a not infrequent and excruciatingly painful complaint, was thought to be caused by vitamin deficiency, from a lack of fresh fruit in the diet. Samuel Pepys was successfully operated on for it.

Below, left: 86. Patrick Lamb's *Royal Cookery* (1710) was distilled from fifty years in the royal kitchens. Besides recipes, Lamb gives layouts for presenting dishes *à la française*, in elegant displays entirely covering the table. Many French recipes had by now become integrated into traditional English fare.

Below, right: 87. *The Queen-like Closet* by Hannah Wolley was published in 1670. Unlike the court cookery books, it was not only written by a woman but also, despite its title, aimed at housewives.

received one four years earlier. On a second occasion, in August 1668, Evelyn is actually standing inside the rail behind Charles at dinner, and describes the dessert served to the king – a pineapple – as the first he has ever seen. Perhaps he means tasted, however, because 'His Majesty having cut it up, was pleased to give me a piece off his own plate to taste of', in which Evelyn was somewhat disappointed, comparing its flavour to quince or melon. Charles II enjoyed fruit, although the food served to him and the court still consisted mainly of a wide array of meat dishes; many courtiers, with no such natural liking as the king's, might have eaten little fruit or vegetables at all (fig. 85).

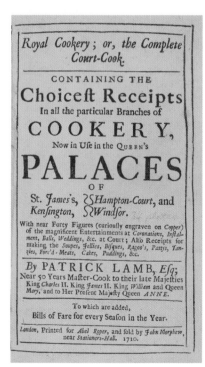

A rash of cookery books appeared after the Restoration (fig. 87). Robert May's *Accomplish't Cook* appeared in 1660 and reflects its author's years in France, as does *The Whole Body of Cookery Dissected* (1661) by William Rabisha, who cooked for the king in exile. *The Closet Opened* (1669) was written by Sir Kenelm Digby, Chancellor to Queen Henrietta Maria in France. It is a homely book; in the recipe for medicinal mead, for example, the boiling time is regulated by the saying of an *Ave Maria*. It also contains recipes for Henrietta's bouillon, barley cream and Portuguese eggs. Patrick Lamb began as a Child of the Pastry for Charles II and ended up as his Master Cook, in which position he continued into the reign of Queen Anne (1702–14). His

88. The anecdotal knighting of the loin of beef. 'Whilst Charles his royal trencher piled/ From one huge loin of beef/ Quoth Charles 'Odd's fish! a noble dish,/ Ah, noble made by me!/ By kingly right, I dub thee knight/ Sir Loin henceforward be.' (Anon.)

influential cookbook, *Royal Cookery*, was published in 1710, after his death (fig. 86).

The great affliction to health during the reign of Charles II was the Black Death, the great plague that decimated the population of London, notably in 1665. Many foods were held responsible for its appearance, and there were many superstitious beliefs about how to avoid catching it. The court had the most sensible idea, one of avoidance, by simply getting out of London to uninfected areas, as James I had done in 1603. Moving between Salisbury and Oxford in July 1665, Charles was given what amounts to a packed lunch, consisting of beef, pullets, pigeons and 'chickes' put into loaves. Was this the first royal chicken sandwich?

Charles II appears to have enjoyed good health until his final year, and one has only to look at his portraits to see that he was a man with a huge appetite for life. He loved witty company, women, fine food, the theatre and parties. One sees him as in a series of flash photographs: being struck by the voluptuous figure of a girl selling oranges at the theatre; spotting a family likeness in her handsome sister seen selling oysters on the street; newly wed Charles and Catherine eating cherries on a summer's day on the queen's gilded balcony at Hampton Court; the king stopping for a quick syllabub from the dairymaid with her cow in St James's Park; dining raucously with the jockeys at Newmarket; getting the stuffy young

89. James II's coronation banquet of 1145 dishes, prepared by Patrick Lamb, was illustrated by Francis Sandford and published in 1687 as the Glorious Revolution was on the horizon, if not yet on the Devonshire coast.

90. William III's Private Dining Room at Hampton Court Palace is laid out for dessert. William loathed dining in public, or even with his sister-in-law, Anne. His 'vulgar behaviour' severely annoyed her when he finished off a dish of green peas without passing it to her, as she had desired.

William of Orange so drunk at dinner that he broke all the windows in the bedchambers of the Maids of Honour; being in on the prank to offer a syllabub prepared with horse urine to the snuff-stealing lofty and loutish Lord Lauderdale; supping elegantly with the Duchess of Mazarin at her home in Chelsea.

The anecdotal knighting of the loin of beef has been variously attributed to Henry VIII, Elizabeth I and James I. The levity of the episode, however, its French play on words – the *surlonge*, a cut above the loin – and the existence of a contemporary verse make its most likely originator Charles II (fig. 88).

The king's very last meal included a goose egg or two, followed on waking the morning after by a China orange and a glass of sherry.

A little later he lost consciousness, but it was nothing to do with the digestibility of goose eggs; the king was suffering kidney failure and had had a stroke, from which he died four days later, despite the painful and intrusive attentions of his doctors.

From Sauerkraut and Sausages to Temperance and Frugality

'A leg of mutton and his wife,
The chief pleasures of his life.'

Peter Pindar on George III

91. Detail from *A Dinner Party* by Marcellus Laroon the Younger, 1725; see fig. 96.

Sundays and Thursdays are public dining days for the royal family in the early eighteenth century. The table is laid in the Public Dining Room with two linen tablecloths and silver cutlery (fig. 92). A succession of covered silver-gilt dishes is brought to the table by liveried servants and offered on bended knee to senior members of the royal family (see the menu on page 98). Today, Sunday 31 July in the year 1737, George II (1727–60), Queen Caroline, their family and the court are at the summer palace of Hampton Court. A Prussian nobleman, Charles-Louis, Baron de Pöllnitz, had visited London a few years earlier, in 1733, and watched the royal family dine:

Their Majesties dine in public upon Sundays when none eat with 'em but their children. The table is in the form of an oblong square in the middle of which sit the King and Queen with the Prince of Wales on the right and the three eldest princesses on the left. The table is placed in the midst of a hall, surrounded with benches to the very ceiling, which are filled with an infinite number of spectators.

The great crowd this Sunday may have reminded the king of how he had laughed when, one day in that very room, the rail surrounding the table, under pressure from the horde of gawping visitors, had given way, causing onlookers to fall over and

92. The Public Dining Room at Hampton Court Palace. George II and Queen Caroline were the last monarchs to live at Hampton Court. Until 1737 they and their children regularly dined in public in this room during their summer months of residence.

scrabble about on the floor to recover their hats and wigs.

Today the Princess of Wales dines with the king and queen and the princesses Emily and Caroline, but Frederick, Prince of Wales does not accompany the princess as once more he is not on speaking terms with his parents. Although he is thirty years old and married, and his wife, Augusta, is expecting their first child, he is treated as a silly adolescent by George II and Queen Caroline, although admittedly he sometimes behaves like one. He seems to be especially silly at mealtimes, insisting on precedence (an armchair for himself, stools for his siblings) at table; gobbling down great glasses of jelly at his wedding feast, while winking at his friends that he is fortifying himself with an aphrodisiac;

bombarding a castle-shaped cake with sugar plums at the time of the Jacobite rebellion; or merely languidly throwing bread rolls.

Dinner this very hot Sunday at the end of July is a most tedious business, and it seems to be going on forever. Pigeons, rabbits, geese, partridges and quails have gone off in the warm weather, and hang stinking in the wet larder (fig. 93). Is it really only 5 o'clock? Princess Augusta is feeling more and more unwell. Another pickled oyster and she will throw up … . She remembers with embarrassment how she was sick all over the queen's shoes at their first meeting, and how she heaved her stomach up at her wedding feast. These memories are not helping her now. At last, very late at night, she gets back to her own apartment and to a sulking Frederick. He is overjoyed at seeing his poor wife in labour, which is what her discomfort

soon reveals itself to be. Now he can be his own man, without interference from his bossy father, who has insisted that the baby be born in whatever palace the king happens to be in at the time. Frederick and his friend the dancing master make arrangements. Between them they heave Augusta down the back stairs into a carriage and drive like the blazes to St James's Palace, where an hour later, between two tablecloths (no bedlinen being prepared), a baby is born. She is named Augusta, after her mother, and will in turn become the mother of Caroline of Brunswick, that wayward, reviled,

unhappy, uncrowned queen of George IV. Tiny Augusta is described by her grandmother on her first viewing later that morning as a 'little rat of a girl about the bigness of a good large toothpick case'. Soon she will be the elder sister of the future King George III. Hello Hanoverians, the British royal family of the eighteenth century.

The birth of Frederick and Augusta's first child and their flight to St James's was the catalyst for a huge row with George II and Queen Caroline, during the course of which the king turned son, daughter-in-law and newborn

93. *Mayhem and Mania in the Culinary Engine-Room*, 1702. Without the aid of refrigeration, food soon went off in the heat of the kitchens. In the royal kitchens in England, women were not generally appointed until the very end of the eighteenth century.

94. Georgian cooking regularly takes place in the restored Prince of Wales's kitchens at Kew. Here the cooks are working at the charcoal range, frying pork and preparing a chocolate tart using original eighteenth-century recipes.

95. Frederick and Augusta might have enjoyed using the Banqueting House, built by William III in the gardens at Hampton Court and decorated by Antonio Verrio, or the Queen's Private Dining Room (shown here), but they were denied lodgings in the palace after 1737.

grandchild out of their apartments at the royal palaces. They were never to re-occupy them. This event echoed an almost identical episode when Frederick's parents, as Prince and Princess of Wales, had been kicked out of the royal palaces by George I.

Frederick and Augusta now acquired a house in Leicester Square, but they lived for the most part in the White House, their little, but lavish, home designed by William Kent at Kew in south-west London. It was there that their children, including their second child, the Prince of Wales (the future George III, 1760–1820), spent many childhood years.

Frederick might no longer live in a royal palace, but he and Augusta had taste and knew how to entertain in style. Elaborate silver Rococo tableware, engraved with the prince's

arms, was commissioned from the English silversmith George Wickes and later from the French goldsmith Nicolas Sprimont. From 1738, this exquisite silver, together with Meissen and Dresden china, was ferried by barge up the River Thames from London to Kew, where Frederick had built himself a state-of-the-art new kitchen next door to the White House (fig. 94). It was fitted with all the latest gadgets, from a copper carp pan to a spice box with partitions and an integral nutmeg grater. Frederick, Prince of Wales dined in admirable style – and totally beyond his means (figs. 95 and 96).

Dining in public was now old hat. This younger generation wanted to be seen fraternizing with poets, musicians, politicians and wits. The poet Alexander Pope, who lived in Twickenham, came to dinner, as did James Thomson, a resident of Richmond and author of the popular poems *The Four Seasons*, and George Lyttelton, poet and politician (and nephew of Lord Cobham of Stowe in

96. Marcellus Laroon the Younger, *A Dinner Party*, 1725. At dinners at the White House, the table was set with services of silver-gilt or Meissen. Even the pats of butter were impressed with the Prince of Wales's feathers, leaving guests in no doubt that this was a royal table.

97. This pair of silver-gilt salts was designed in the form of a crayfish on a clam shell by Nicolas Sprimont for Frederick, Prince of Wales in about 1742. The prince had a similar pair made in the form of crabs with conch shells.

Buckinghamshire), was attached to the household.

The poor short-lived Frederick died in 1751, and the Dowager Princess, now a single mother of eight, dined as best she could. That proved to be remarkably well. The amazing Augusta, who had arrived in England aged sixteen, clasping her doll and without a word of English, had, under Frederick's tutelage, developed interests in the natural sciences, arts and gardening. Dinner invitations found her seated with men of letters, discussing the

98. In the eighteenth century, the royal kitchens purchased cucumbers by the thousand for making sauces. Samuel Johnson thought 'a cucumber should be well sliced, and dressed with pepper and vinegar, and then thrown out as good for nothing'.

problems of shocking electricity or planning her gardens at Kew, bringing down rumours of scandal on the inquisitive lady's innocent head. When a live turtle was delivered to her kitchen at Kew, she immediately sent over the Thames for her Clerk of the Closet, the learned Dr Stephen Hales, author of numerous scientific tracts and a dab hand at making ice cream for royal dinner parties. He came hotfoot to dissect the turtle on the kitchen table, before the remains of the poor animal were scooped into the cooking pot (fig. 99).

Compared to the stuffy atmosphere of the court, his mother's establishment was a stimulating environment for the young Prince of Wales. Although he would lack some of

99. Frederick's kitchens at Kew retain many original features from their fitting out in 1738: the elm table on which the poor turtle must have been dissected, spits, smoke jack, charcoal ranges and small oven all date from the eighteenth century.

100. *Halte de chasse* was painted in 1737 by Charles-André van Loo for the private apartments of Louis XV at Fontainebleau. It depicts exactly the kind of fashionable picnic Frederick, Prince of Wales would have enjoyed with friends and family, on birthdays and other occasions, by the River Thames at Richmond.

101. *Change of Diet; A Ballad: being a Sequel to the Roast Beef of Old England*, 1757. The English took pride in plain English cooking and distrusted French cuisine with its rich sauces, complicated recipes and outlandish ingredients. The Englishman John Bull is shown to thrive on his diet; his French counterpart is invariably thin and sickly.

the social graces he might have acquired at court, he developed a great interest in country affairs and agriculture, leading to his nickname of 'Farmer' George. His interest in food production, however, was a serious one. He superintended his farm at Richmond, where he set about improving the national flock by introducing merino sheep from Spain, and he was always on the lookout for new methods of animal husbandry and grain production. Under the name Ralph Robinson of Windsor, he contributed to debates on such matters in the *Annals of Agriculture*.

As a child George had been terrified of his uncle, the hugely fat William, Duke of Cumberland, nicknamed the 'butcher of Culloden' after his harsh treatment of the Scots Jacobite rebels in 1746. Augusta may occasionally have hinted darkly that, given the chance, Cumberland would not hesitate to seize the throne. One day William mentioned to George that a propensity to put on weight ran in the family, and told him quite squarely that if he did not severely curtail his diet, George would end up as grotesquely obese as himself (see fig. 127). This remark left the young man stricken with horror, and from that moment he embarked on a course of moderation, if not frugality. If anything, this increased as George grew older. It was perhaps just as well that public royal dining had all but died out, since there was now little to see.

For breakfast the king might have a dish of tea. Dinner, until his illness of 1788, would be taken with the queen and princesses at about 4 pm, followed by a buffet supper at 11, at which he lightly grazed before bedtime. Neither was Queen Charlotte (whom he married in 1761) a great eater, and she was described as picking at dishes rather than ever eating a whole plateful of food (fig. 102).

102. James Gillray, *Temperance Enjoying a Frugal Meal*, 1792. George III enjoys a boiled egg, while Queen Charlotte has a plate of salad. It was true that the king was abstemious, but the queen was hardly as avaricious as portrayed here.

103. Queen Charlotte with the Prince of Wales and Prince Frederick, by Johann Zoffany, *c.* 1765. The princes' childhood diets were strictly regulated. As part of their education they learned to plant crops and bake bread.

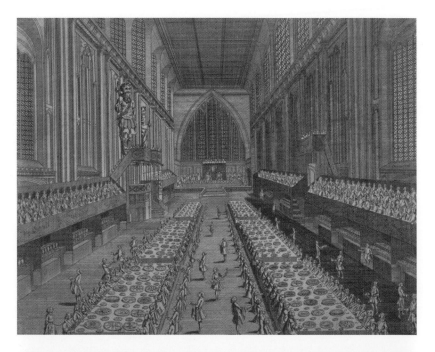

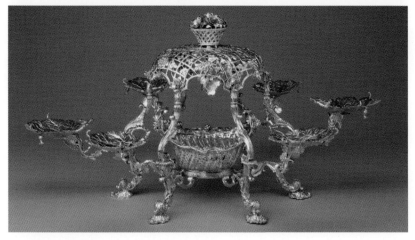

Despite their own preferences, as king and queen George and Charlotte were expected to preside over splendid banquets. Accordingly, the young king ordered from the goldsmith Thomas Heming a silver-gilt dining service, which became known as the Coronation Service, although it was not finished in time for the coronation banquet. It consists of more than ninety plates, seventy-two serving dishes and other items, including an elaborate epergne (fig. 105). It was put into use for the magnificent banquet given for Christian VII of Denmark at the Queen's House (later known as Buckingham Palace) in 1768, although for most of George III's reign it saw more of the inside of the silver vault than of candlelit dinner tables.

Later in his life, after a day's journey from Windsor, attending a levée, meeting countless people and dealing with a mass of paperwork, George III would eat only 'a few slices of bread and butter and a dish of tea', according to the memoir writer Sir Nathaniel Wraxall. And it was not just food that George regulated. In 1786 Fanny Burney recounted a complaint of the king's equerry: '"Here Goldsworthy, I say!" he cries, "Will you have a little barley water?" Barley water in such a plight as that! Fine compensation for a wet jacket, truly! – Barley water! I never heard of such a thing in my life! Barley water after a whole day's hard hunting!'

Top: 104. The Guildhall is prepared for the reception of George III and Queen Charlotte at the Lord Mayor's Day banquet in 1761. All the dishes are laid out on the tables *à la française*, so that guests may help themselves.

105. This silver-gilt epergne (1762) by Thomas Heming is the centrepiece of the Coronation Service ordered by George III. It was also the most expensive item, costing £241. 19s.

Their usual breakfast is milk in a bason, two thirds milk and one of tea moderately sweetened and dry toast of the statute bread … their dinner, soup if they chuse it, when not very strong or heavy and any plain meat without fat, of one sort, clear gravy and greens, of which they eat what they please. Fish when they please, but without butter, using shrimps, strained from the sauce or oyl and vinegar. As the second course they eat fruit of the tart without the crust, peas or what other simple thing they chuse, but of one only. At the desert, they eat ice of one sort they chuse … coffee was allowed only on those two days or one glass of any sort of wine they chuse after dinner – repletion will give to the Prince of Wales the symptoms of a smart fever which is totally prevented if His Royal Highness is pleased to have a general attention to the quality and quantity of his food.

Given the control exerted by both the king and the queen over their own diet, it was not surprising that they attempted to regulate the diets of their children (fig. 103). Before they reached the age of five, George's two eldest sons were subjected to a strict regime, as their tutor, the Duke of Montagu, described:

As His Royal Highness was only four years old, the choice of diet and its application obviously originated with his parents. It was reported that the king and queen regularly breakfasted with their children, and frequently 'amuse themselves with sitting in the room while the children dine … Exercise, air and light diet are the grand fundamentals in the King's idea of health and sprightliness; his majesty feeds chiefly on vegetables, and drinks little wine; the queen is what many private gentlewomen would call whimsically abstemious; for at a table covered with dainties, she culls the plainest and the simplest dish, and seldom eats of more than two things at a meal.'

Despite the queen's faddy eating habits and the king's known preference for a little plain-cooked mutton, vegetables and barley water, the cooks of the royal household kept producing, day after day, the elaborate meals worked out by the Master Cook and the Clerk of the Kitchen (fig. 107). Dinner consisted of three courses or removes, each of eight or nine dishes, starting with soup and a variety of meats and vegetables, progressing to a large roast with all the trimmings, and ending with a medley of savoury and sweet dishes. This bill of fare was served up even during the period of the king's so-called 'madness' in 1788–89, when, Fanny Burney tells us, Queen Charlotte sat with her head in her hands for most of the day and took so little nourishment that her stays were falling off her (Burney was, after all, her dresser and should have known). The king, who at the end of December was thought likely to die, spent many days in the strait waistcoat, and was forcibly fed at most a mouthful or two of soup at a time.

By mid-January 1789, the king's condition had begun erratically to improve. As part of his treatment, he was regularly given asses' milk, and vomits and emetics in jellies and wine, and on Friday 16 January, the clergyman brother of

Dr Willis (the king's physician) relates, the king 'ate three jellies and puked heartily again'. He was withheld a knife and fork until 6 February, however. It is surprising, then, that the following bill of fare was served to 'Their Majesties' table', as recorded by the Clerk of the Kitchen in his ledger for Friday 16 January 1789:

THE FIRST COURSE

Soupe santé
2 capons à la croute
A ragout, 2 breasts
8 cutlets de mouton
Une langue de bœuf
1 pullet, petit patties béchamel
7 salmon, anchovy sauce
3 aspic of chickens
13 loin of veal smort [veal in butter sauce]

THE SECOND COURSE

Portland mutton roasted
8¾ lb of neck of mutton

THE THIRD COURSE

3 partridges roasted
2 wild ducks roasted
2 almond cakes creamed
Asparagus
Pancakes
Galantine [stuffed poached meat]
Tart
Maccarony
Broccoli
Blancmange

Dinner, served at about 4 pm, was followed by a late supper of two pullets 'à la maitre

107. The Clerk of the
Kitchen inspects food
being delivered to the
royal kitchens to check
that its quality, freshness
and quantity are in line
with the payment being
made.

d'hôtel', roast potatoes, a tart, 'schollars eggs, 3 soles en marinade, spinnage, ribs of lamb roasted and two chicken broth'.

This is hardly a diet for an invalid, and certainly it was not the king and queen who ate all this food. The elder princesses and their ladies-in-waiting might have picked at it, but that would scarcely have made a dent in this extravagant royal meal. It was not the equerries; they were served up an almost identical dinner and a supper of larks, tarts, whiting, endives and cold pheasant at their own tables, as were the king's and queen's pages, who had cods' heads, roasted capon, venison pasty, 20 lb of boiled mutton and tart for their lunch that day, followed by a supper of veal, cold chicken and omelette. The kitchen staff, footmen, grooms, dressers, doctors and servants all received a substantial dinner of roast meat every day, and little Princess Amelia came over to the White House for dinner, with her governess and servants, from the nearby house in which they were staying. Chicken sandwiches were made in large numbers, and there was a very generous allowance of 14½ lb of beef and 29¾ lb of veal for soup. What happened to the food that did not end up in the royal stomachs?

At the beginning of George III's reign, William, Earl Talbot, the Lord Steward, had undertaken a thorough inquiry into the operation of the royal household, particularly the kitchen, the staff of which was subsequently reduced almost by half. New regulations were brought in for the payment of bills and the ordering of provisions; exact procedures for the purchase, delivery, use and disposal of supplies were pinned up in the Clerk of the Kitchen's office; and the kitchen staff were obliged to sign an oath of loyalty. However, as had previously occurred, a gradual reversion to unacceptable waste, exaggerated perquisites and the deviation of food to those not officially entitled to it slowly eroded the retrenchment, so that by

1780 the 'Great Reformer' Edmund Burke MP was again calling for reductions to be made in the royal kitchens. He suggested that contracting services to those skilled in kitchen management would produce better economic results. The situation was a complex one, however, and it would be another hundred years before the matter was addressed more satisfactorily, by Prince Albert (see page 155).

Interestingly, Mrs Papendiek, wife of the page to the three eldest daughters of George III, recorded from her own experience that any

108. Drawing by Thomas Rowlandson of George III's discovery of a louse on his plate. In the 1770s Peter Pindar turned this adventure into a mock-heroic epic entitled *The Lousiad*. Following the incident, the king supposedly ordered all his kitchen staff to shave their heads.

would positively allow no more. Enraged at the unexpected and unroyal disappointment, he furiously put his hand in his pocket, took out sixpence, sent out a page for two pennyworth of pippins, and received the change.'

Among those managing the kitchens in the 1780s were experienced and well-established staff. Clerk of the Kitchen William Gorton was a former tax inspector. He was perhaps a little over-fond of puddings, but he certainly kept the accounts in apple-pie order. Master Cook William Wybrow was a middle-aged and well-respected chef who had been employed in the king's kitchens since he was a boy of eight. These were not people likely to countenance food racketeering. Against all the regulations, however, food was finding its way out of the royal premises and into hungry mouths, although these were no longer officially waiting at the palace gates.

Another likely destination for the uneaten royal food was reuse within the household itself. Only the royal family and their personal attendants were served supper. Those who were not probably ate leftovers that would otherwise have gone to waste. Suppers were usually cold buffets, and it is likely that roast chickens, for example, served at dinner might be brought out again. Menus for the following day's dinners could also make use of leftover food in such composed dishes as ragouts, gallimaufry, minced pullet and collop (meat) pies.

109. The Master Scourer in the Royal Kitchens earned an excellent wage, but his job was extremely onerous. Copper pans had to be thoroughly scoured with sand to eliminate any debris, which could lead to the formation of verdigris. Dishes were washed with lye, a strong alkaline solution.

food for the princesses' table remaining untouched would be brought home by Mr Papendiek, but anything already tasted he would allow his servant to take. Peter Pindar (the pseudonym of the satirist John Wolcot) commented that the kitchens were so tightly run that, on one occasion, when George III asked for some apples he particularly liked, he was 'informed that the Board of Green Cloth

Reheating food was, of course, not without its dangers. According to Mrs Papendiek, in 1785 a Windsor chef preparing an official dinner inadvertently killed nineteen diners, 'many of them even before they could reach their homes', through his desire to prepare an unforgettable meal. He got up extremely early to stew a turtle, but fell asleep and let the fire go out. When he woke up, he reheated the turtle soup without removing it from the pan, a circumstance that resulted in the formation of verdigris on the inadequately tinned copper (fig. 109).

110. An eighteenth-century baker puts rolls into a bread oven using a long-handled peel, or shovel. Good, wholesome bread was baked every morning for the royal household.

Boulanger.

Nor was the danger all out in the dining room. Chefs, including the famous Antonin Carême, succumbed to years of low-level ingestion of carbon monoxide from charcoal ranges, where they stood for hours stirring soups, sauces and ragouts. High levels of carbon monoxide in poorly ventilated kitchens could very quickly cause fainting, unconsciousness and sometimes even death. The poor of the country cooked in iron pots over an open fire and so escaped both these forms of poisoning, but there were other dangers lurking in food to which all were subject.

The writer Tobias Smollett described a 'deleterious paste, mixed up with chalk, alum and bone-ashes, insipid to the taste and destructive to the constitution'; those purchasing it called it 'bread'. This was not the only food to have cheap and harmful added ingredients: it was found that pickles acquired a lovely green tint with a drop of sulphuric acid, which was also useful for making vinegar. Chalk was used to whiten and thicken skimmed and watered-down milk, and cheap tea might have dust, lead or other substances added to the twice-used leaves. Legislation against food adulteration was in place, but the means of testing food, especially in poorer districts, were inadequate to deal with the level of contamination.

Not that the king had any such worries. His tea, which he drank with the queen at 8 pm as the regimental band played on the terrace at Windsor, was of the finest. His food was ordered from the most prestigious suppliers, who boasted of being in the king's service, thereby attracting other wealthy customers. In the 1780s, regular suppliers were mostly in London, but they delivered to all the palaces, usually weekly but also daily if required. The supplier of jellies was one Anne Wickles, who had inherited the business from her widowed mother, Elizabeth. Her jellies came at sixpence the glass, or two shillings for a large one to share. The man delivering herbs and roots – or vegetables – at this time was a greengrocer by the strange name of Savage Bear, who brought bunches of watercress by the dozen, asparagus and French beans by the hundred, apples by the bushel and mushrooms by the pottle (punnet).

Meat was still the preferred food, and English roast beef was judged to be the finest in the world. A Swedish visitor to London sums up a much-voiced opinion of the time:

> *English meat whether it is of ox, calf, sheep or swine, has a fatness and a delicious taste, either because of the excellent pasture, which consists of such nourishing and sweet scented kinds of hay as there are in this country where the cultivation of meadows has been brought to such high perfection[,] or some way of fattening the cattle known to the butchers alone[,] or for some other reason. The Englishmen understand almost better than any other people the art of properly roasting a joint, which also is not to be wondered at, because the art of cooking as practised by most Englishmen does not extend much beyond roast beef and plum pudding.*

More than 3500 lb of beef and 2500 lb of mutton and veal were ordered by the court during one month alone in the late 1780s, although this must refer to carcass weight and not butchered meat. However, every part of the animal could be, and was, turned into nourishing dishes: bones, ribs, neck, breasts, tail, guts, sweetbreads, fryes (testicles), liver, heart, tripe, tongue and 'gangs' (pairs) of ears and feet. A good proportion went into making gravy and soups, too. Head was a delicacy, and a scalded calf's head was the essential ingredient for mock turtle soup. Meat was cheap: beef and mutton cost 4½d./lb, and pork and veal sixpence. Poultry was more expensive, at 1s. 6d. for a good-sized chicken and six shillings for a turkey. Fish was the most expensive, with salmon and cod at 2s./lb and a good-sized turbot costing anything up to £1. 10s. Fish, particularly cod or skate, was often crimped – slashed to the bone just before or after being killed – to make the flesh firmer. Larks were roasted by the dozen for the princesses' dinner, and, besides game birds, other small birds were commonly on the menu,

111. Charles Williams,
The Honors of the Sitting!!
A Cabinet Picture, 1805.
George III dines with
Henry Addington. The
king was very fond of his
former prime minister, and
gave him the title Viscount
Sidmouth. They sat down
together on at least two
occasions to a dinner of
mutton and pudding.

including blackbirds, starlings, knots and
godwits, and others that have unsurprisingly
become extinct. Butter was extremely
expensive at 11½d./lb, but it was used
extensively in cooking. Many foods were
seasonal, which affected their price, quality
and availability. Italian foods were gaining
in popularity by the third quarter of the
eighteenth century, with Parmesan cheese,
vermicelli and macaroni appearing regularly

on the monthly grocery orders of the Clerk
of the Kitchen.

The meat allowance in the royal household
must have been in the region of 4–6 lb per
person per day. This seems excessive, although
bone, gristle and fat were included in the
figure. Lean meat was, however, not always
the most popular, or considered to be the
most tasty. The advice given to young people
by the Revd John Trusler in his book of 1791 on

112. In this painting of 1771 by John Atkinson, a cook surveys his list of ingredients. The royal cook's recipes had to be within the guidelines set by the Clerk. Although the 'abstemiousness and frugality' of George III were admired, by 1779 it was 'necessary to introduce not only economy but parsimony into the Royal Kitchen' (*Public Advertiser*, 13 July 1779).

the rules of behaviour during meals gives an insight into the shift of taste over two centuries. Between the initial chapter, mentioning a 'new mode' of seating – 'a gentleman and lady sitting alternately round the table', which he describes as 'promiscuous seating' – and the final, heavily moralizing chapter ('shew in every thing a modesty') is a fascinating section on the art of carving, updated for the late eighteenth century, from which may be glimpsed what was then popular taste. Among other instructions, Trusler gives advice for carving a calf's head, which he describes as 'a genteel dish':

> When first cut, it should be quite along the cheek bone, in the fleshy part, where many handsome slices may be cut. In the fleshy part, at the end of the jaw bone, lies part of the throat sweet-bread, which may be cut into and which is esteemed the best part in the head. Many like the eye, which is to be cut from its socket by forcing the point of a carving knife down to the bottom on one edge of the socket, and cutting quite round, keeping the point of the knife slanting towards the middle, so as to separate the meat from the bone. This piece is seldom divided, but if you wish to oblige two persons with it, it may be cut into two parts. The palate is also reckoned by some a delicate morsel … . There is also … some nice, gristly fat to be pared off about the ear … . There is a tooth in the upper jaw … called the sweet-tooth … [it] may readily be taken out with the point of a knife. … In serving your guest with a slice of head, you should enquire whether he would have any of the tongue or brains, which are generally served up in a separate dish.

Calves' heads – not a dish to appeal to the squeamish of our times – were then considered a delicacy, and were not infrequently on the menu for the king and at other royal household tables. They would almost certainly not have been relished by the next king, however. It was perhaps during the regency and reign of George IV that a shift in royal taste came about, possibly inspired by his preference for all things French. His early desire for fine foods and sophisticated dining was far removed from the simple tastes his father had so painstakingly tried – and failed – to instil into his eldest son, whose ever-expanding gourmet enjoyments were to prove his undoing.

The King of Cooks Meets the King of Gluttons

'Georgie Porgie pudding and pie,
Kissed the girls and made them cry.
When the bills came in to pay,
Georgie Porgie waddled away.'

Variation on a well-known nursery rhyme

113. James Gillray, *A Voluptuary Under the Horrors of Digestion*, 1792. The heir to the throne, George, Prince of Wales, picks his teeth with a fork after an enormous meal. Gillray's portrayal of royalty, particularly George IV, was merciless. George tried to buy off caricatures he found particularly offensive, but he was not always successful.

In July 1816 the 'king of cooks', Antonin Carême, was lured from Paris to London to be chef for the Prince Regent, the future George IV (1820–30; fig. 113). In 1792, as an abandoned eight- year-old waif at the height of the Terror in Paris, Carême had been scooped off the street by a *gargotier*, a greasy-spoon cook in a downtown eatery, looking for a skivvy. The young Carême set to work in earnest, with his eyes on the stars, and through his own self-discipline, determination and hard work had by 1804 opened a fashionable patisserie. Along the way he educated himself in architecture at the Bibliothèque Nationale, wrote cookbooks and cooked for the foreign minister, Talleyrand, and on occasion Napoleon, and he was now steadily rising to become the most innovative and celebrated chef in Europe (fig. 114). The Prince Regent, on the other hand, born on a satin cushion, was at that time languishing in his long-awaited Regency, gout-ridden, filling the day with trifles and fripperies, putting on weight at an alarming rate and being unsuccessfully steered by his doctors towards a simpler, healthier diet of plain boiled vegetables and barley water. 'Carême, you will kill me with so much food', the Prince Regent was heard to say to the lured chef. 'I want to eat everything you cook – the temptations are just too great.' 'Monseigneur,' the cook was heard to reply, 'through the variety of my dishes, it is my job to stimulate your appetite; it is not my job to restrain it.'

114. At the height of his profession, Antonin Carême worked for royal and noble families across Europe, but he always longed to return to Paris. Beginning as a patissier, he made himself master of all forms and wrote several cookery books.

From his own background of rigid self-control, the cook's attitude to *gourmet* and *gourmand* was thus clearly defined. The Prince Regent, too, had his own attitude; he was clearly a glutton, but strictly a gourmet glutton. Carême did indeed provide a surfeit of food, but in an effervescence of gastronomic imagination, delighting equally the palate and the eye. Every dish was the most exquisite work of art in its own right. It was to be a lethal combination for the Prince Regent.

On 19 June 1811, before the luring of Carême, George had invited 2000 guests, including the whole exiled French royal family and nobility, to dinner in the Gothic Conservatory at his lavishly decorated and gilded London residence, Carlton House, hung for the evening with blue silk and fleurs-de-lys (fig. 115). The new Regent was dressed not in the trappings of royalty but with all the accoutrements of a field marshal (military uniforms had always been his favourite dress, although he had never been allowed to venture near a battlefield). On this particular evening, one of his attendants outdid even the Prince's fantasy by appearing in 'a complete suit of ancient armour', according to the writer

115. A squeeze at Carlton House in 1811. More than 2000 people were invited to the Prince Regent's fete. Carlton House was then opened to the public, so that they could view the interiors. The crush was so great that a number of people were injured, and many more lost hats and shoes.

116. The Gothic Dining Room at Carlton House, by Charles Wild, 1817. Designed by John Nash in 1814, the room featured eight enormous crystal chandeliers. The Regent's vast collection of silver-gilt plate was displayed on shelves around the room and in tiers at the far end.

Robert Huish, although what function the man performed is not stated.

The Prince Regent never needed much prompting to hold a party. That held in June 1811, it was generally assumed, was a celebration of the Regency, which had been put in place four months earlier; although the *Gentleman's Magazine* firmly announced the event to be a benefit for British artists and, as an afterthought, a remembrance of the king's birthday on 4 June. The august parent was unfortunately unable to attend, since he was now spending his time conversing with imaginary persons in a locked suite of rooms at Windsor, where *his* supper consisted of cocoa, tea and jellies.

117. This silver-gilt dessert stand by Paul Storr and Philip Rundell is one of a set of four with figures representing the seasons, purchased by the Prince Regent. Much of the plate ordered at this time still looks stunning on the royal table at banquets held today.

The guests began assembling at 9 pm, when they were given an opportunity to marvel at the newly completed interiors of Carlton House. The Prince Regent welcomed the French royal family at 10 o'clock, after which they too were given the tour, reported by the *Gentleman's Magazine* to be 'devoid of all ceremony', while in the background the bands of the three regiments of Foot Guards and the Prince Regent's own band, all in full dress uniform, played a medley of marches.

When finally dinner was called, at 2.30 am, there was a scramble for the 200 officially ticketed places. The Prince Regent sat at the head of a 200-foot table, down the middle

of which ran a murmuring stream of water, spurting in cascades from a silver fountain, with aquatic flowers and gold and silver fish, while along its mossy banks his guests dined off silver-gilt plates. Lord Colchester, who had squeezed into the banquet without a ticket, commented: 'My children would have been amused with the river of water and the little gudgeons swimming about in the whole length of the table, and all the grown children were equally delighted.' Behind the Regent's plain mahogany dining chair, Colchester continued, had been erected a buffet or sideboard three storeys high, glistening with gold plate – vases, urns, salvers – 'the whole surmounted by a Spanish urn, taken from on board the "invincible Armada"' (fig. 118).

The food seemed to take second place to the general entertainment, and was hardly commented on. It consisted for the most part of hot soups and roasts, prepared by the Master Cook, George Rawlinson (most definitely an Englishman), who had been inherited with the Regency. As the evening was extremely warm, the array of cold dishes proved more popular. There was a lavish display of fruit, including pineapples, grapes, peaches and strawberries, and the champagne flowed freely. It was reckoned that the evening cost in the region of £120,000.

At a time when most people in England were struggling through the effects of war to find enough to fill their bellies, this excess did not go unnoticed. The poet Shelley commented with accuracy that this would not be the 'last bauble which the nation must buy to amuse this overgrown bantling of Regency'. Indeed, immediately the party was over, the fledgling Regent set off for Ludgate Hill to order from Rundell, Bridge & Rundell a Grand Service of silver-gilt plate; it eventually extended to more than 4000 pieces and would finally cost George and the taxpayer over £60,000 (fig. 117).

Until this time, the royal kitchens had generally employed only men; now, at last, Carlton House admitted a woman, Mary

Morton – at first employed as a kitchen maid – into the kitchen establishment (fig. 119). At £40 per annum, she was on a reasonable salary, although when she progressed to being a pastry cook, she was still paid only £50, and the first woman cook in the royal kitchens (appointed the following year) earned only £58, compared to the £80 paid to male cooks. Two women crept into the confectionery, again paid scaled-down rates of £61 and £40. But it was a start. Armand Vilmet, a Frenchman, took over the role of Master Cook, with Francis Le Clerc as his pastry cook. The latter earned the staggering salary of £221 per annum,

119. Before the end of the eighteenth century, only men worked in the royal kitchens, apart from a few female pudding-makers. In this view of the St James's Palace kitchens by James Stephanoff, published in 1819, women are now chopping ribs of beef and helping to load the spit.

probably to entice him from the Leveson-Gower household, where he had been previously employed.

In July 1814, with Napoleon seemingly securely imprisoned on the Italian island of Elba, the Duke of Wellington triumphant at the Battle of Toulouse, and the Treaty of Paris signed, the Regent considered it time for another grand fete, this time in honour of Wellington. Tsar Alexander I of Russia, Frederick William III of Prussia, Count Platov and Field Marshal Blücher arrived in London

to join the premature victory celebrations, and the Regent invested Louis XVIII with the Order of the Garter. Elaborate buildings were constructed in the gardens of Carlton House: a rotunda and a Corinthian temple, and supper tents hung with white and rose curtains and decorated with the regimental colours on silk. More than 2000 guests were invited, and the Prince Regent appeared as their field marshal, complete with garter, sash and star. Even Queen Charlotte joined the company, which sat down to supper at 2 am.

120. During the Prince Regent's fete in 1814, the Chinese pagoda in St James's Park, lit with gas, caught fire, and two men and several swans were killed. The crowd, unaware of the reality of the disaster, thought it capital entertainment.

This was followed the next week by the London Parks Gala in celebration of the centenary of the Hanoverian accession, with yet another jamboree of buildings: a seven-storey Chinese pagoda and four yellow bridge pavilions with bright blue roofs in St James's Park; a 100-foot Gothic castle in Green Park; Hyde Park turned into a fairground with booths, stalls, arcades, swings and roundabouts, and the Battle of the Nile re-enacted as a regatta on the Serpentine; and the Mall hung with coloured lanterns. 'The most brilliant fireworks ever seen in this country' (*Morning Post*, 1 August 1814) unfortunately burned down the Chinese pagoda (fig. 120). It was all considered part of the festivities celebrating 'the Triumph of England under the Regency'. Queen Charlotte afterwards invited a carefully chosen 300 people to join her at a banquet at the Queen's House.

Between 1814 and the luring of Carême in 1816, events moved swiftly on the European stage. Napoleon dramatically re-emerged from Elba, sweeping France into the disaster of the Battle of Waterloo in June 1815, while the Prince Regent, personally in debt to the tune of over £550,000, found that 'playing at king is no sinecure'. This realization, combined with an unfortunate spraining of his ankle during a spirited demonstration of the Highland fling, left him out of sorts and in the growing grip of alcohol and laudanum addiction in an anguished attempt to dull mental anxiety and physical pain.

Not that this seemed to affect the Regent's appetite for food. He had a strict protocol for dining. His own pages in their dark-blue livery trimmed with gold lace stood behind his chair, handing him whatever he asked for and taking his dirty plates. The dishes for each course were still laid out on the table at the same time, and diners helped themselves; the Regent was helped by his pages to anything he fancied. This extended his choice to whatever dish was on any part of the table, unlike the other guests, who were limited to the dishes in front of them. After the removal of the second tablecloths, when the epergne of fruit and the cheese boards were taken away, wine was set out for more concentrated all-male drinking

121. A view by John Nash of the Banqueting Room at the Royal Pavilion, Brighton, 1824. It is uncertain whether this room, designed by Robert Jones, was completed in time for Carême's banquet of January 1817. The Regent is shown sitting centre right.

and serious conversation. Meanwhile coffee, tea and liqueurs were served in the drawing room to the ladies. The recently introduced 'promiscuous' practice of seating ladies and gentlemen alternately at table, replacing the long lines of men and women seated strictly according to rank, meant that segregation by sex was now relegated to the end of the meal, when the ladies were removed entirely to

a separate room (although something very similar had informally been in place since ancient times).

The long wars were truly over by 1816, Napoleon having been decisively defeated on the battlefield of Waterloo and exiled further afield to the lonely outpost of St Helena in the South Atlantic. It was certainly a propitious time for the Prince Regent to invite his

122. *Costumes parallèles du cuisinier ancien et moderne*, 1822. The figure on the right is thought to be Carême, in the costume he designed for the new-style cook. It included the toque, a tall stiffened hat, a version of which is still worn by chefs today.

allies for yet another grand banquet and fete, and to entice the chef of the great Talleyrand and the fallen Napoleon to England. What a contrast for Carême: from Napoleon, the indifferent nibbler, to the Prince Regent, the greedy gourmet.

In November 1816 Grand Duke Nicholas, the future Tsar Nicholas I of Russia, came to England. Wishing to see new British industry, he enthusiastically toured the manufactories and fisheries of north-eastern England and Scotland. The Prince Regent, whose interests centred more on the newly purchased Elgin marbles and Sir Thomas Lawrence's commissioned portraits for the new Waterloo Chamber at Windsor, invited the Grand Duke to Brighton to show off his nearly restored pavilion and impress him with food cooked by the new chef. The great Carême's former role as cook to Napoleon provided a slight frisson and the excuse for yet more toasts to victory, thoughts of which still exercised the royal imagination. That the Russian army had been hundreds of miles away from the Battle of Waterloo was irrelevant to the Regent, who, in his haze of laudanum, was beginning to believe that he had personally led the attack on the battlefield.

The kitchens of the Royal Pavilion at Brighton were already completed, and the adjacent Banqueting Room with its onion-dome roof and large Chinese panels was

a magnificent dining room, even in its unfinished state (fig. 121). Although he was now building in oriental style, George had been a Francophile from a young age, purchasing French furniture, Sèvres porcelain and art. It was therefore not surprising that French cuisine was also to his taste and the cooks he employed were very largely French. In Carême, he finally had the greatest cook of the age, and he was looking forward to introducing him to the most up-to-date, gadget-laden kitchen of the day (fig. 122).

The kitchens and their offices occupied more than a quarter of the ground-floor space of the pavilion, and had pumped water,

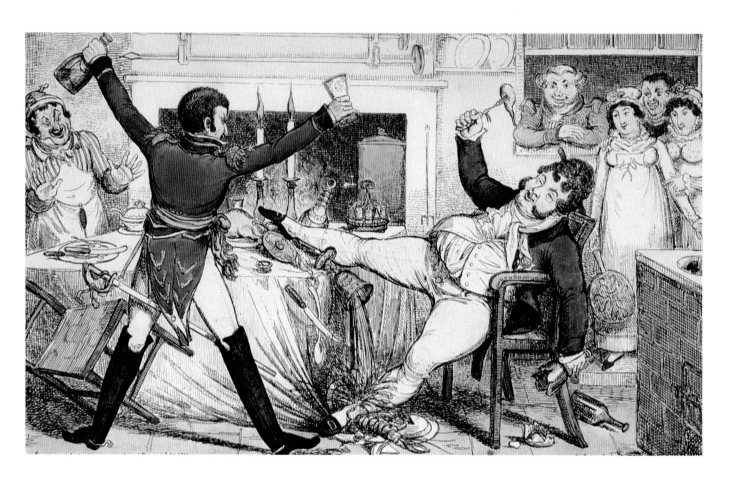

123. Robert Cruikshank, *High Life Below Stairs*, 1819. The Prince Regent regales himself at dinner in the kitchen of the Royal Pavilion 'for the edification and amusement of the Cooks, Scullions, Dishwashers, Lick-trenchers, Shoe-blacks, Cinder-sifters &c'.

meat larders, a bake house, an extra-large ice room and two pastry and three confectionery offices. The prince was so pleased with his new kitchens that he included them on the personal tours he gave to his guests, and on at least one occasion he himself sat down to dinner in the Great Kitchen (fig. 123).

Full use had been made of the discovery of the moment, which was revolutionizing the country: steam. In the main kitchen, a 14-foot-long oval table with cast-iron top heated with steam had largely resolved

the problem of how to keep food hot when serving *à la française*, whereby up to thirty dishes were put on the table simultaneously in an elaborate arrangement. The warming-table meant that all those dishes could now be kept hot while they waited to be taken to the dining room. It was put to full use when the Prince Regent entertained the Grand Duke on 18 January 1817. This is the menu that Carême prepared and served on that evening:

DINNER SERVED AT
THE ROYAL PAVILION AT BRIGHTON
TO HIS ROYAL HIGHNESS THE PRINCE REGENT
AND GRAND DUKE NICHOLAS OF RUSSIA

8 SOUPES
EIGHT SOUPS

Les profitralles de volaille
à la moderne
Chicken and mixed vegetables

Le potage santé au consommé
Clear consommé

Le potage de mouton à l'anglaise
Soup of mutton with capers

Le potage de riz à la Crécy
Rice soup with carrot

Le potage de pigeons à la marinière
Pigeon soup

Le potage de karick à l'indienne
Curried chicken soup

Le potage à la d'Orlèans
Consommé with chicken
quenelles

Le potage de céleri consommé
de volaille
Celery soup – fowl consommé

8 RELEVÉS DE POISSON
EIGHT REMOVES OF FISH

Les perches à la hollandaise
Perch in hollandaise sauce

La truite saumonée à la Génoise
Salmon trout served
Genoese style

Le cabillaud à la crème
Cod in mornay sauce

Le brocket à l'espagnol garni
de laitances
Pike garnished with its roes

Les soles au gratin et aux truffes
Breaded sole with truffle garnish

Le turbot, sauce aux crevettes
Turbot in shrimp sauce

Les merlans frits à l'anglaise
Fried whiting with diced vegetables

Le hure d'esturgeon au vin
de Champagne
The head of a great sturgeon
in Champagne

40 ENTRÉES
FORTY ENTREES SERVED
AROUND THE FISH
(ARRANGED AROUND THE FISH DISHES AS INDICATED)

La santé de poulardes à la d'Artois
Spring chickens

Les ris de veau glacés à la chicorée
Glazed veal sweetbreads with chicory

La croustade de grives au gratin
Tart of thrushes au gratin

Les poulets à la reine, à la Chevry
Chicken à la Chevry

Les côtelettes de lapereaux en lorgnette
Young rabbit cutlets

(LES PERCHES À LA HOLLANDAISE)
Les quenelles de volaille en turban
Quenelles of young fowl in cockscomb
and mushroom sauce

Les cailles à la mirepoix, ragôut à la fiancière
Quail with diced vegetables

La magnonaise de perdreaux à la gelée
Jellied partridge with mayonnaise

L'émincé de langues à la Clermont
Sliced tongue with cabbage
and chestnuts

Les poulets dépecés l'Italienne
Diced chicken in ham and
mushroom sauce

(LA TRUITE SAUMONÉE À LA GÉNOISE)

Les filets de volaille en demi-deuil
Fillets of game fowl in white sauce

Les aiguillettes de canards à la bigarade
Sliced duck in bitter orange sauce

La darne de saumon au beurre
de Montpellier
Salmon steaks in Montpellier butter

Le pain de volaille à la royale
Mousse of game fowl with cream
and truffles

Les filets d'agneaux à la Toulouse
Fillet of lamb garnished with kidneys
and sweetbreads

(LE CABILLAUD À LA CRÈME)

La caisse de lapereaux au laurier
Rabbit pie with bay leaves

La blanquette de poulardes aux champignons
Spring chicken in creamed
mushroom sauce

La casserole au riz à la Monglas
Rice casserole with truffle
and foie gras

Les petits canetons à la Nivernoise
Braised ducklings with lettuce

Le sauté de faisans à la Périgord
Sautéed pheasant in foie gras sauce

Les sautés de perdreaux au suprême
Supremes of pheasant in
white sauce

Le chevalier de poulets garni d'Orly
A crown fashioned of chicken in
tomato sauce

La timbale de nouilles à la polonaise
Timbale of pasta with boiled egg
and asparagus

Les escalopes de chevreuil à l'espagnole
Escalope of venison with fried onions
and tomatoes

Les ballotines de poulardes à la tomate
Pullet galantine in tomato sauce

(LES SOLES AU GRATIN)

Les bécasses, entrée de broche
à l'espagnole
Spit-roasted woodcock

Les filets de volaille à la belle vue
Chicken in aspic

Les hateletes d'aspic de filets de soles
Fillets of sole in warmed aspic

Les cervelles de veaux à la milanaise
Fried veal brains with a Parmesan crust

Les escalopes de gélinottes, sauce salmis
Escalopes of grouse in game sauce

(LE TURBOT, SAUCE AUX CREVETTES)

Les filets de poulardes glacés
aux concombres
Glazed chicken fillets with
braised cucumber

Les boudins de faisans à la Richelieu
Pheasant sausages in Madeira sauce

La salade de volaille à l'ancienne
Chicken salad with onions

La noix de jambon aux épinards
Cushion of ham on a bed of spinach

Les ailerons de poulardes à la Piémontaise
Risotto of chicken wings
and white truffle

(LES MERLANS FRITS À L'ANGLAISE)

Les pigeons au beurre d'écrevisses
Pigeons in crayfish butter

La poularde à la maquignon
Chicken in a gypsy style

Le vol-au-vent à la Nesle, Allemande
Pastry nests in white sauce

Les côtelettes de mouton à la purée
de pommes de terres
Mutton chops with creamed
potatoes

Les filets de poulardes à la Pompadour
Poached chicken in aspic glaze

15 ASSIETTES VOLANTS À SERVIR
APRÉS LES POISSONS
PLATTERS AFTER THE FISH

De petits vol-au-vents à la reine
Chicken vol-au-vent

De petit pâtés de mauviettes
Terrine of larks

De croquettes à la royale
Chicken rissoles

De canetons à la Luxembourg
Ducklings Luxembourg

De filets de poissons à l'Orly
Battered fried fish
in tomato sauce

EIGHT GREAT PIECES

Le quartier de sanglier mariné
Marinaded haunch of boar

Les poulardes à l'anglaise
Pullets with diced vegetables

Les filets de bœuf à la Napolitaine
Fillets of beef with horseradish,
ham and Madeira

Les faisans truffés à la Périgueux
Pheasants in truffle and
wine sauce

La dinde à la Godard moderne
Turkey garnished with kidney,
sweetbreads and vegetables

La longe de veau à la Monglas
Loin of veal with truffle, foie gras
and pickled tongue

*Les perdrix aux choux et
racines glacées*
Partridges with cabbages
and glazed roots

Le rosbif de quartier de mouton
Roast mutton

8 PIÈCES MONTÉES
EIGHT CENTREPIECES PATISSERIE, ARCHITECTURES IN SPUN SUGAR, FONDANT AND MARZIPAN

Un Pavilion italien
An Italian pavilion

Un Ermitage suisse
A Swiss hermitage

La grosse meringue à la Parisienne
Great Parisian meringue

Croque-en-bouche aux pistaches
Tower of caramelized profiteroles
with pistachios

Un Ermitage gallois
A Welsh hermitage

Un Pavilion asiatique
The Royal Pavilion rendered
in pastry

Un gros nougat à la française
A great nougat in the
French style

Croque-en-bouche aux anis
Tower of profiteroles
with aniseed

8 ROASTS
EIGHT ROASTS

Les bécasses bardées
Woodcock larded with bacon

Le dindonneau
Turkey

Les faisans piqués
Spiced pheasants

Les poulardes au cresson
Chicken with watercress

Les sarcelles au citron
Teal dressed with lemons

Les poulets à la reine
Chicken with truffle tartlets

Les gélinottes
Grouse

Les cailles bardées
Quails larded with bacon

32 ENTREMETS
THIRTY-TWO DESSERTS AND
SAVOURY ENTREMETS
(OF WHICH SIXTEEN ARE DESSERTS,
WITH INDICATION OF ARRANGEMENT
AROUND ROASTS AND CENTREPIECES)

Les concombres farcies au velouté
Stuffed cucumber in white sauce

La gelée de groseilles
Conserve of redcurrants

(LES BÉCASSES BARDÉES)
Les gaufres aux raisins de Corinthe
Greek raisin waffles

Les épinards à l'anglaise
Buttered spinach

(LE PAVILION ITALIEN)
Le buisson des homards
A pyramid of lobsters with
fried parsley

Les tartelettes d'abricots pralinées
Apricot and almond tartlets

(LE DINDONNEAU)
La gelée de marasquins fouettée
Upside-down maraschino jelly

Les œufs brouillés aux truffes
Scrambled eggs with truffle shavings

(LA GROSSE MERINGUE À LA PARISIENNE)
Les navets à la Chartres
Turnips in tarragon sauce

Le pouding de pommes au rhum
Apple and rum pudding

(LES FAISANS PIQUÉS)
Les diadèmes au gros sucre
Spun sugar diadems

Les choux-fleurs à la magnonaise
Cauliflower in mayonnaise

(L'ERMITAGE SUISSE)
Les truffes à la serviette
Truffles in warm linen

Les fanchonettes aux avelines
Chicken, chicory and hazelnut salad

(LES POULARDES AU CRESSON)
La gelée de citrons renversé
Lemon jelly with whipped cream

La croute aux champignons
Mushroom tart

Les cardes à l'espagnol
Artichokes à l'espagnol

La gelée de fraises
Conserve of strawberries

(LES CAILLES BARDÉES)
Les gateaux renversés, glacés au gros sucre
Upside-down cakes with
caramel glaze

Le buisson de crevettes
Pyramid of shrimp

(LE PAVILION ASIATIQUE)
La salade de salsifis à l'italienne
Salsify salad

Les gateaux à la dauphine
Dauphine cream cake

(LES GÉLINOTTES)
Le fromage Bavarois aux abricots
Apricot blancmange

Les laitues à l'essence de jambon
Lettuce in ham liquor

(LE GROS NOUGAT À LA FRANÇAISE)
Les champignons grillés demi-glacé
Grilled mushrooms
with sherry

Les pannequets à la Chantilly
Pancakes with Chantilly cream

(LES POULETS À LA REINE)
Les pains à la duchesse
Almond loaf

Les truffes à la serviette
Truffles in warm linen

(L'ERMITAGE GALLOIS)
Les pommes de terre à la Lyonnaise
Sautéed potatoes with parsley

Les gateaux d'amandes glacés à la rose
Rose fondant almond cakes

(LES SARCELLES AU CITRON)
La gelée de cuirassau de Hollande
Orange liqueur jelly

Les céleris à l'espagnol
Braised celery

12 ASSIETTES VOLANTES
TWELVE GREAT ROUNDS

4 soufflés de pomme
Four apple soufflés

4 soufflés à la vanille
Four vanilla soufflés

4 fondus
Four fondues

124. Detail from a view by John Nash of the Great Kitchen at the Royal Pavilion, Brighton. It was hot work for the two cooks whose job it was to keep the fire well stoked and to roast meat and poultry on the spit.

125. A drawing from Antonin Carême's *L'Art de la cuisine française* for presentation of his lobster dishes. The savoury *pièces montées* often feature exquisite morsels attached with decorative skewers, by which means the guests may help themselves.

Possibly the highlight of the dinner were the *pièces montées* for which Carême, the Palladio of posh palatial puddings, was rightly famous. These eight centrepieces in spun sugar, fondant and marzipan each represented a style of architecture; there was even a pastry version of the Royal Pavilion. Each stood some 3 feet high and was very accurately detailed. Temperature was vital to the survival of these fragile pieces; the most miniscule change, or a slight breeze from an open door or window, could cause hours of work to collapse into sticky ruins in seconds. They also had to be extremely carefully handled, of course. Carême had already created eight great architectural

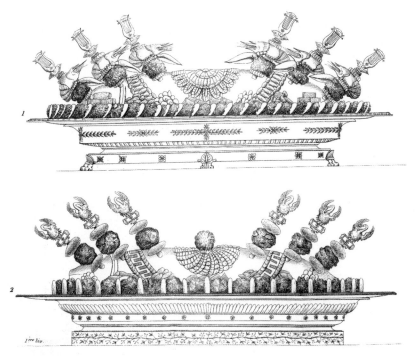

pièces de pâtisserie for a dinner held by the Regent three days earlier.

How Carême cooked so much food to such a high standard, and presented it so beautifully, remains a mystery. A condition of his coming to England had been that he would be allowed enough time to continue writing his magnum opus, *L'Art de la cuisine française* (fig. 125). He thought previous cookbooks were mediocre and full of mistakes, and considered that English food, apart from its beef, had little to recommend it. Following Voltaire's maxim 'a good cook is also a fine doctor', he boasted that his cooking had cured the Prince Regent's gout. Sentiments of this nature can hardly have endeared him to the Regent's regular cooks.

126. The medieval royal kitchens at Windsor Castle are still in use today. This view by James Stephanoff shows them in 1817. In the foreground meat is being weighed before being allocated and spit-roasted for those entitled to eat at royal household tables.

After eight months, Carême declared: 'Mon âme toute française ne peut vivre qu'en France' ('My French soul can live only in France'); but perhaps it was rather the bad feeling in the kitchen and the envy of the royal household staff that drove him back to France.

Carême might have been tempted away by Grand Duke Nicholas at Brighton. Almost immediately after returning to Paris, he left for St Petersburg to cook for the wedding of the duke to Princess Charlotte of Prussia. The Prince Regent would have been intrigued by a new kitchen gadget in St Petersburg, enabling a fully laden table to rise from the kitchen to the diners in the room above. This complicated Russian mechanism would not have been required, however, for Carême's new invention, the vol-au-vent, which needed only a breath of air to waft it to the table.

The Regent had been and could still be an excellent host, and he continued to give his annual children's party, a ball at Carlton House. However, his charm might suddenly evaporate as he went into delusional overdrive, effusively telling guests how idolized he was by his subjects.

As Grand Duke Nicholas must have seen in his travels through the country in the midwinter of 1816–17, people were experiencing the worst food shortages for many years. The year 1816 was described as the year without a summer, because of a volcanic eruption on an island far away in the Indian Ocean. The amount of dust in the air may have produced

the most beautiful sunsets ever seen for Turner to paint, but it also caused frost in June and driving, freezing rain, which left the sodden and unripe wheat rotting in the fields. There was little bread to be had, or afforded where it was available, and there were food riots up and down the land. Ten days after his most splendid dinner at Brighton, an attempt was made on the Regent's life as he travelled by carriage from Carlton House to the State Opening of Parliament.

It is hard to see how the Prince Regent had travelled so far from the great promise shown in his early years, but much was attributable to lack of control over his purse, his indulgences and his diet. Great things had been expected of George III's firstborn son. The prince's first memory, he later recounted, was at the age of three, when his great-uncle William, Duke of Cumberland 'took me in his arms and placed me on his knee where he held me a long time. The enormity of his bulk excited my wonder' (fig. 127). Interestingly, at the same age little Princess Victoria had a very similar memory of George himself, or 'Uncle King', as she called him, made worse by the fact that he kissed her with his grease-painted lips.

George's early life had been one of regimentation, but it was not devoid of affection from both parents, who were busy breeding for the nation. 'A constellation of delight!' exclaimed Gainsborough as he

128. The nearest George IV came to a Grand Tour was sending his Clerk of the Kitchen, factotum and Westphalian gingerbread maker, Louis Weltje (pictured here in 1781), to Paris to buy porcelain and furniture. Weltje also hired chefs and negotiated the purchase in Brighton of the Marine Pavilion, which was to become the Royal Pavilion.

129. Drawing by Antonin Carême from *Le Pâtissier pittoresque*, 1842. Carême reproduced in sugar the architectural wonders of the world, which the Regent was unable to visit. Fine eating formed a fantasy life – although its consequences of ill health and debt were far from illusory.

benefited greatly later on from a Grand Tour, which would have enriched both his personal and intellectual life, and the crown (figs. 128 and 129). Turning instead to overindulgence, particularly during such lean times of war and hardship for his countrymen, meant that the Prince Regent was both ridiculed and despised. Nor did the Regency style for tight-fitting breeches help his image. The Regent had become the Prince of Whales (fig. 130).

painted George's fourteen siblings. On her way to see the old Princess Amelia, Lady Mary Coke, a friend of the royal governess Lady Charlotte Finch, frequently dropped in to see her as she breakfasted with the royal children at Kew. Lady Mary recalled her conversations with the precocious four-year-old Prince of Wales, whom she thought 'the most comical child I ever saw'. On one visit he offered her a slice of melon from his plate, and on another he was rather out of humour because it was not his 'meat day', enquiring in a low voice 'whether it was Princess Amelia's meat day'.

The little Prince of Wales was a promising child of many talents, and would have

THE PRINCE OF WHALES OR THE FISHERMAN AT ANCHOR.

130. *The Prince of Whales,*
1812: George Cruikshank
most memorably pictured
him; Charles Lamb wrote
about the Prince Regent:
'Not a fatter fish than he/
flounders round the polar
sea/ see his blubbers – at
his gills/ what a world of
drink he swills.'

The death in November 1817 of the Regent's
only daughter, Charlotte, in childbirth, and of
her male child, devastated parent and dynasty.
As George increased his intake of laudanum,
George's brothers married German princesses in
a race to produce an heir to the throne. George
himself gave away the brides and arranged a
wedding breakfast for the dukes of Clarence and
Kent and their new duchesses at Kew Palace in
July 1818. This modest meal consisted of turtle
soup, fish and venison, melons, pineapples,
grapes and peaches. Queen Charlotte was too
ill to attend the wedding breakfast, and a few
months later she died, followed after fourteen
months by old George III. At the age of fifty-
seven, the Regent was finally George IV, and
began his plans for a resplendent coronation
ceremony and banquet.

Just before the coronation, George IV
dined with his sister Princess Augusta at the
Berkshire estate of Frogmore, which had been
left to her in her mother's will. She commented
on how 'dreadfully dejected and thoughtful'
her brother looked, until he began to eat, 'but
when he dined, [and] ate as much as would
serve me for three days ... together with a bottle
of strong punch, he was in much better spirits
and vastly agreeable'.

George IV's coronation banquet in 1821
was the last of its kind (fig. 131). As had so
many newly crowned kings before him, the
exhausted king sat in Westminster Hall,
to which Caroline, his estranged wife, but
uncrowned queen, had hysterically but
unsuccessfully attempted to gain admittance
a few hours earlier. Uncharacteristically, the

king toyed with some turtle soup, a dish of quails and a slice of capon, and left the hall when the party was in full swing. The peers of the realm then tucked into soup, salmon, turbot, trout, venison, veal, mutton, beef, capon, lobster, crayfish, cold roast fowl and lamb, potatoes, peas, cauliflower, pastries, jellies and cream, while their famished families looked down on them from the galleries. Occasionally a chicken leg or two in a napkin would be tossed up to the onlookers. Dinners of roast beef and plum pudding were handed out to the poor of London, and the evening finished with fireworks in Hyde Park.

The king, in the grip of gout, recurrent bladder infections, growing obesity, failing eyesight and frequent shortness of breath, now made a pitiful figure of majesty. At 20 stone, he was too many inches a king. His medicine was largely cherry brandy, downed in such quantities as 'not to be believed' (according to the Duke of Wellington). He became a recluse, threatening servants with dismissal if they looked at him. When he did venture out, he painted his face with greasepaint and covered his head with a wig.

As the 1820s came to a close, the king spent more and more time in bed. His doctor, Sir William Knighton, said he got up to have dinner only when his mistress Lady Conyngham was there. Otherwise he would doze, when he was not ordering food – chicken,

cherry brandy, punch, pastries. The Duke of Wellington reported that for his breakfast in April 1830 the king had been served 'a pidgeon and beef steak pie, of which he eat [sic] two pigeons and three beef-steaks, three parts of a bottle of Mozelle, a glass of dry champagne, two glasses of port and a glass of brandy. He had taken laudanum the night before [and] again, before his breakfast.' Any dietary advice from his doctors fell on deaf ears, although George had already convinced himself that he was eating an ordered diet and taking regular exercise. Throughout his many ailments, he never seemed to lose his appetite. The king's sister Mary, Duchess of Gloucester described her brother as 'enormous, like a feather bed', and on his feather bed at Windsor Castle the king died just after a quarter past three on 26 June 1830.

Talleyrand commented: 'King George IV was a "roi grand seigneur" ... there are no others left.' *The Times*, however, reported: 'Never was an individual less regretted by his fellow men than this deceased king.' Most unfair. He certainly was a prince of excellent taste, but unfortunately taste led to appetite; appetite to indulgence; and indulgence to overindulgence. The temptation was just too great. Perhaps food per se did not destroy George IV, but – as Carême had so wisely surmised – the king needed to play his part in curbing his appetite. That, lamentably, he could not do.

131. George IV's coronation
banquet in Westminster
Hall in 1821 was the last
grand coronation banquet
ever held. The King's
Champion rode into the
packed hall, and hundreds
of dishes were served.
The new king, unusually,
seemed to have lost his
appetite, and only picked
at his food.

Shoot It, Hang It, Stuff It, Scoff It

'Every meal is a lesson learned.'
Victorian proverb

132. Detail from *Evening at Balmoral Castle* by Carl Haag, 1853–54; see fig. 143.

'The day has come and I am alone', began Queen Victoria (1837–1901) in her journal entry for the fiftieth anniversary of her accession, her Golden Jubilee on 20 June 1887 (fig. 133). After breakfast at Frogmore amid thoughts of loneliness and her dear Albert, the sixty-eight-year-old queen took the train from Windsor to London Paddington, and travelled through jubilant crowds to Buckingham Palace where most of the crowned heads of Europe were awaiting her arrival for luncheon, an enormous one even by Queen Victoria's standards. It was held at a huge oval table in the large dining room, which had not been used since Albert's death. The queen was escorted into lunch by the King of Saxony. After lunch she gave a series of audiences until 4.30 pm, after which she took tea in the garden with princesses Beatrice and Helena, before dressing for the large 'family' dinner. The family by this time included many European monarchs, and they sat down to dinner in the supper room, which (the queen wrote in her journal) 'looked splendid with the buffet covered with the gold plate' (fig. 135). This medieval display continues at royal banquets to this day.

The Princess of Wales's father, King Christian IX of Denmark, sat on Victoria's right, and the princess's brother, 'Willy' (King George I) of Greece, on her left at the large horseshoe-shaped table, brilliant with candles illuminating the uniforms of the men and

THE ROYAL ARMS JUBILANT.

the gorgeous gowns of the ladies. After dinner, as the queen's band played in the ballroom, Victoria managed to slip away to the comfort of her room.

The following day, after a service of thanksgiving and a triumphal drive of all the visiting royalty through the city, the queen prepared for another grand dinner, again in the supper room at Buckingham Palace. Victoria, who sat between the king of Denmark and her cousin King Leopold II of the Belgians, wore diamonds and a dress embroidered with silver motifs of the rose, thistle and shamrock. Lunch started with a choice of three soups, including turtle soup; moved on to fish, lamb, duck, asparagus, beef, venison, chicken, green beans and foie gras; and finished with pancakes, cherry pudding and profiteroles. Cold joints of beef, tongue and chicken were an extra on a side table. At the end of the meal, as the toasts were proposed, pipers with swirling kilts and skirling bagpipes swept into the room and paraded around the table, giving the signal for the party to move into the ballroom. The queen, by this time 'half dead' with fatigue, had herself 'rolled back' to her room as soon as she was able to slip away.

Ten years on, Queen Victoria was the first monarch to celebrate her Diamond Jubilee. It was a magnificent but scaled-down version of the event of 1887 for the seventy-eight-year-old queen, who came up from Windsor, as she had

Top: 133. Tom Merry, *The Royal Arms Jubilant*, June 1887. Queen Victoria's Golden Jubilee was celebrated throughout Great Britain and the Empire with parties, fireworks and a plethora of souvenirs.

134. Princess Alexandra gave Jubilee meals in 1897 for the 'deserving poor' of London. This dinner held in the People's Palace in Mile End consisted of bread, roast beef and two vegetables, jelly, pastry and lemonade, with an orange for every child.

135. Jubilee Banquet, 20 June 1887, held in the Ball Supper Room at Buckingham Palace, by Robert Taylor Pritchett, 1887. Queen Victoria described in her journal the guests present and the appearance of the table and buffet, but made no mention of what she ate.

a decade earlier, to lunch with her family at Buckingham Palace. In the evening she sat between Archduke Franz Ferdinand and the Prince of Naples at a celebration dinner, arranged on twelve 'little' tables, as Victoria described them, in the supper room. This was another 'family' meal, in a manner of speaking, for by this time the queen's family, through astute marriage and copulation, had populated almost all the royal palaces of Europe. There was slightly less choice on the menu than in 1887, but its preparation was perfection, aided by twenty-four French chefs brought specially from Paris. The young Swiss Gabriel Tschumi, who entered the kitchens at Buckingham Palace the following year as an apprentice and went on to become Master Chef to Victoria, Edward VII and George V, remembered hearing

136. Giant, ornate cakes were made for Queen Victoria's Golden and Diamond jubilees. The official jubilee cake of 1897 weighed 1000 lb, including decoration. Wreathed in red roses, it sprouted monograms, medallions, crowns, lions, unicorns, angels of fame and glory blowing sugar trumpets, and an angel of peace with white shining wings.

about the making of the *Rosettes de saumon au rubis* (salmon rosettes in ruby jelly). The claret jelly for this dish was prepared by one of the French chefs, but not to the exacting standards of Monsieur Ménager, Queen Victoria's head chef, who complained that 'a good jelly should be like a drop of whisky, quite clear, without the slightest cloud in it … then *make* the claret jelly as clear as whisky', which the chef duly did.

There remained the 15-foot-high Jubilee cake to be eaten, but the queen was already suffering from dyspepsia and exhaustion. Across the Channel, in a tastelessly papered hotel room in Paris, a lonely Oscar Wilde celebrated the Jubilee with fifteen French gamins, singing 'God Save The Queen' and the 'Marseillaise' and sharing a large pink sugar cake wreathed in red roses and inscribed 'jubilée de la reine Victoria'.

Traditionally, until now, even the grandest of banquets had been laid out on the table so that the guests could help themselves. Over the course of the eighteenth century, the layout had become an art form in its own right. It necessitated at least two tablecloths, both of which were laid on the table at the beginning of the meal. The cook would have planned how the dishes were to be displayed, balancing foods of different types with their colour and form both to achieve an attractive table layout and to offer each guest a variety of dishes. Of

course, not everything by any means would be within reach of each guest. The options were for the guest to ask for a dish to be passed or to content him- or herself with the dishes to hand. At a royal dinner, inhibitions were certainly greater than in a less formal situation, yet the variety of food on one's plate depended on cultivating a rapport with one's fellow diner, otherwise the meal might be very frugal indeed.

As one course ended, the dishes were removed and replaced by those for the next course. Until about the end of George IV's

137. When meals began to be served *à la russe*, every guest was served with the same menu. The table should have been less cluttered, but flowers, lighting, decorations and expanded place settings with new items – such as fish knives and forks – soon filled the gaps.

reign, sweet dishes were still included in the first and second courses. Large joints of meat would be carved at a sideboard and brought to the table. After the first two courses the top tablecloth was removed and the dessert, arranged with artistry, served on the clean cloth. Sculptures in sugar and ice fitted perfectly into this mode of service, known as *service à la française,* and fruit was often displayed in a silver epergne or in pierced and patterned silver bowls or trays.

One can immediately see the advantages and pitfalls of such a manner of serving. In its

favour, the food is seen as being plentiful and beautifully presented; in theory guests can help themselves to whatever and however much they want; and it encourages conversation among guests. But there is little room on the table for anything but food; you may very much want a dish but not have access to it; and since all the food for each course has to be served at the same time, hot dishes are likely to be eaten lukewarm.

From the mid-nineteenth century, *service à la russe* was gradually adopted in large establishments, including the court, and it is still in general use today (fig. 137). Food is arranged on individual plates in the kitchen and served by waiters, usually over the diner's left shoulder, with vegetables and sauces brought in waves in the same manner. This left room on the table for candelabra and flowers, although each place setting increased in size because of the ever-increasing number of knives and forks required, including such new cutlery as fish knives and forks. The downside was that fewer people could be seated around a table and a large staff was required, which, if it included clumsy servers, could result in sauce splashed down the left-hand side of a new designer gown. Queen Victoria's mention of 'little' tables at the dinner of 1897 almost certainly means that the meal was served *à la russe*.

'We are not amused!' Whether this phrase ever actually issued from the royal mouth as Queen Victoria sat surveying her guests down the long table at Windsor, or whether diners were simply stopped mid-sentence by a censorious look from the slightly hooded royal eye, is unclear. In any case, the queen's meaning was plain. For a guest already nervous at being in royal company, it was the dinner-party conversation stopper par excellence. Surprisingly, the queen tolerated a great deal of liberal dinner-table conversation. She liked to hear of good practical jokes, was amused by mimicry (at which she herself excelled) and was

tolerant of drunkenness in those she favoured, but her mood could change abruptly, and sexual innuendo or immorality were always frowned on.

As for her consumption of food, Queen Victoria was a gobbler all her life. Whether this was habit, greed, a general lack of interest in food or a disinclination to spend time at the table, it demonstrated to the people dining with her, and to the royal cooks, a lack of appreciation of the food being served (fig. 138). Many slowly eating guests must have gone home hungry and disappointed, as protocol dictated that when the royal knife and fork were finally laid on the plate, all those at the table were also required to end their meal. In the normal course of the day, Queen Victoria expected dinner – which began in the early part of her reign at 8 pm, and later moved to 9 – to take up no more than half an hour of her time, even though it involved at least four courses, beginning with soup, followed by fish, roast meat, dessert and fruit. Although Gladstone, a slow eater, and the 'deferential breed' of lords-in-waiting may not have eaten their fill, etiquette did not deter Lord Hartington on one occasion from finishing his mutton and peas. Lord Ribblesdale observed that when 'the mutton was taken away from him, he stopped in the middle of a sentence in time to arrest the scarlet-clad marauder: "Here, bring that back!"' Lord Ribblesdale looked anxiously to the

138. Queen Victoria attends the Guildhall banquet in November 1837. The Lord Mayor's banquet lasted five hours, which the new queen, with her tendency to eat quickly, must have found very trying.

queen, but was amazed to see her smile. On this occasion she was definitely amused. But in a different mood, as a lady-in-waiting reported, the queen might reject a dish with a 'peevish moue ... more eloquent than words'.

Brought up at Kensington Palace under the watchful eye of her mother, the Duchess of Kent, and governess, Baroness Lehzen, Princess Victoria recalled her youthful diet as regular and simple (fig. 139). Mealtimes constituted

the framework of her ordered little life, with breakfast at 8.30, luncheon at 1.30 and dinner at 7. Tea came as a treat in later years. As a thirteen-year-old on a visit to Alton Towers, she dined with the Earl of Shrewsbury and was impressed, not with the food (unmentioned), but with the fact that it was served on 'splendid gold plate'. Her elder half-sister, Feodora, tried to encourage her to eat less, to take more exercise and to stop adding so much salt to her

139. Stephen Poyntz Denning, *Princess Victoria Aged Four,* 1823. The princess's early life was strictly controlled, with regular hours for meals, but she was allowed to eat her bread and milk from a small silver basin at the dinner table if there was no company.

was prescribed for her, with a simple diet of potato soup and a slice of bread and butter for luncheon and mutton with rice for dinner, followed by a dessert of orange jelly. Oranges she loved for the rest of her life, spooning them out from the top, but mutton she always disliked, commenting that when she became queen, she would never have mutton for dinner again. Although mutton broth was frequently on the menu for others, the queen avoided it, preferring fresh lamb from the Welsh hills.

Upon her accession, Victoria exclaimed: 'I have very pleasant large dinners every day. I invite my Premier generally once a week to dinner, as I think it right to show publicly that I esteem him.' Her fatherly prime minister, Lord Melbourne, did not hesitate to warn the new queen, as the old Duke of Cumberland had warned her grandfather George III, and failed to influence her uncle George IV, that the Hanoverians have a tendency to overindulge, and that she was likely to become 'very fat'. He suggested that she eat less and exercise more. She did try, but found that walking made her feet swell, so she took to riding, which gave her an appetite. The 4 ft 11 in. queen was soon having her dresses let out at the waist. Yet a few inches were neither here nor there, and after the reigns of her ancient, overblown uncles the young queen, delighted with her own new life, charmed all those she met. The old politician

food, which sounds eminently sensible advice. Even Leopold I of Belgium wrote of his fourteen-year-old niece that she 'eats too much and almost always a little too fast'.

Towards the end of 1835, Princess Victoria developed what might have been a chronic form of typhoid fever. Her appetite gone, she began to lose weight. A daily dose of quinine

141. Queen Victoria, Prince Albert and their growing children appreciated the privacy afforded by Osborne House on the Isle of Wight, where they enjoyed a private family Christmas. Here they are seen gathered around the Christmas tree – a German import.

Thomas Creevey remarked: 'She eats quite as heartily as she laughs, I think I may say she gobbles … but … she blushes and laughs every instant in so natural a way as to disarm anybody.'

As the young queen discovered love, Albert and sex, her appetite for food may have been curbed for a while, but as the babies began to arrive she seems to have fallen back on her old childhood comfort foods of bread, milk and porridge, food not far removed from the 'beef, potatoes and grog' that she had found so 'excellent' when she had visited Nelson's ship HMS *Victory* at Portsmouth as a teenager. Champagne had always made her giddy, and although she was advised to drink good-quality wine from the unlimited choice in her extensive cellars, she preferred sweet ale or to mix her wine or sherry with sugar and hot water. Victoria was prone to sick headaches and indigestion, for which she tended to blame such foods as turtle soup and pork. Highly spiced foods were more likely to have been the root of the problem, but then the whole household seemed to suffer from stomach complaints. Baroness Lehzen resorted to a diet of potatoes and endlessly chewed caraway seeds to alleviate her discomfort, while Prince Albert's 'delicate stomach' was unbalanced by any kind of emotional upset, of which there was plenty during his life with the headstrong young Victoria.

Family life and nursery food at Osborne House on the Isle of Wight provided the queen with her own brand of happiness (fig. 141). The growing number of little ones ran about to their hearts' content; according to Eleanor Stanley, a lady-in-waiting, 'assisted by their august Papa [they] washed a basketful of potatoes, and shelled a ditto of peas, which they are to cook for themselves today if they are good'. The princesses learned how to cook in a miniature kitchen in the Swiss Cottage in the grounds, purchasing their ingredients from their own miniature grocer's shop, Spratt's, which was supplied by the royal gardeners. For the young queen, it was a royal family idyll: breakfast in the summer house, sketching, writing or riding with Albert, picking strawberries or other wild fruit with the children, taking tea with them in the garden, and having a romantic dinner alone with Albert, followed by a moonlit walk with the beloved, gazing at the sea from the terrace.

When Victoria and Albert discovered Scotland in 1842, the Highland diet proved to be just the queen's cup of tea. Familiar, homely foods with romantic names were exactly what Victoria's contradictory character craved: bannocks, Finnan haddie, neeps and tatties, haggis, crowdie and cloutie dumplings – warming nursery food for grown-ups.

142. No matter how cold it was, there were picnics like this one at Cairn Lochan in the Cairngorms. Usually John Brown had a drop of whisky to keep out the cold. Queen Victoria described this as 'a bonny place'.

143. Carl Haag, *Evening at Balmoral Castle,* 1853–54. Prince Albert shows Queen Victoria and the Prince of Wales the stags brought home from the hunt and laid outside Balmoral Castle in the traditional manner. The queen commissioned this painting for Prince Albert's birthday.

Moreover, there was the wonderful dress of the Highlanders, the pipes and dances, and the fact that the country reminded Albert of his native Germany. Balmoral, rebuilt to Albert's instructions and tartanized, became a *gemütlich* (cosy) nest from which the royal family could go on picnics and exciting, sometimes even hazardous, expeditions (fig. 142). The queen bought Albert a silver luncheon box in which to take out his 'frugal' stalking snacks. He did not on the whole prove very adept at bringing home dinner, however; on one early hunting

expedition, eight of the party fired at the same woodcock, rendering it somewhat inedible, as Lady Eleanor observed: 'If we are to eat it … eight charges of shot is rather too much for one woodcock.' When shooting with Lord Breadalbane at Taymouth, the party bagged nineteen roe deer, several hares and pheasants and three brace of grouse, and wounded a capercaillie. On another occasion Albert left Victoria in order to stalk a ptarmigan, and shot two. The queen revelled in the exotic names of these birds, and claimed that stalking was 'one of the most fatiguing and interesting of pursuits' (fig. 143).

The particular delights of Scotland were perhaps the great expeditions, when Victoria and Albert – with a lady, usually Jane Churchill, and one of Albert's gentlemen, as well as ghillies John Grant and John Brown – set off incognito with horses and carriages to explore the Highlands, staying under assumed names in various inns. The occasions when Brown slipped up and called the queen 'Your Majesty' caused hilarity, although the crown on the dog cart was a sure giveaway, if nothing else. Queen Victoria's report of her first stay at an inn is one of the rare occasions when she writes about food. She had asked Grant and Brown to wait at table, but they declared themselves too 'bashfull'. The party had brought their own wine, which probably had a Windsor label on it, and the notion that it could be put on the table with glasses for one to help oneself, the queen described as 'the old English fashion'. The dinner she thought 'fair and all very clean: soup, hodge-podge [hotpot], mutton broth with vegetables which I did not much relish, fowl with white sauce, good roast lamb, very good potatoes, besides one or two other dishes, which I did not taste, ending with a good tart of cranberries'. For a remote Highland inn to have served up a lavish meal of such complexity must have required great organization, not to mention a little collusion.

In fact, the following morning, after some 'good tea and bread and butter and some excellent porridge', the royal party left the inn and found, to their intense amazement, the whole neighbourhood out waving flags in the street.

On Victoria and Albert's second expedition, a traveller, having arrived at night at the inn, wanted to come into the dining room for breakfast. On being refused entry, he became curious, and again the cat was out of the bag. On the third expedition, the queen was disappointed by her stay at an inn at Dalwhinnie, where she claimed, 'there was hardly anything to eat, and there was only tea, and two miserable starved Highland chickens, without any potatoes! No pudding, and no *fun*'. Grant and Brown had on this occasion been prevailed upon to wait at table, as the queen – a far cry from her seventeenth-century ancestors – did not want any stranger in the room as she ate. After their stint at serving, the poor ghillies, together with all the other servants, found that their own dinners consisted only of what little remained of the two scrawny chickens.

In Ireland at the time, millions of people were starving following the blighting of the potato harvest. Although Queen Victoria personally gave £2000 towards the famine relief, and had a compassionate nature of a sentimental kind – her sensibilities were deeply touched by 'accounts of starvation in the workhouses' after reading *Oliver Twist* – it is doubtful whether she fully grasped either the dire situation in Ireland or the nature of the very great poverty and hunger on her own doorstep in London (fig. 144). Prince Albert had a more realistic and constructive view on these and many other subjects, and was highly regarded by men of substance for his enquiring and well-informed mind, which, it was hoped, would over time inform the queen's sometimes headstrong opinions. Therefore, it was a double tragedy when he succumbed to overwork and typhoid at the end of 1861. The government had lost a highly respected royal voice, and the queen had lost the only love of her life, her partner and the father of her children.

Besides his active interest in politics, science and the arts, Albert had been appalled by the state of the royal household and its operation in Buckingham Palace. He was astounded to find that three completely separate departments, often seemingly at odds with one another, were responsible for the most menial tasks, such as cleaning windows, lighting fires and supplying candles. Some of the appointments were outright sinecures, the work that should have accompanied the nominal post being lost in the mists of time.

144. This is the Public Soup Kitchen that operated in Euston Road from 1846. In winter as many as 550 people each day might come in for a bowl of beef soup, made with ox head.

145. Staff in the kitchen at Windsor Castle prepare Christmas food for the royal family in 1857. The great Christmas pie is sitting in the centre of the large table, ready for serving.

Candle supply was typical of many of the household duties where an outdated method had been retained and perverted to supply perquisites to the performer of the task. When a candle was fixed in place, it could be lit for a second and snuffed out, after which it became the property of the household staff. Pilfering was widespread, and a colossal amount of food either was eaten by those without authorization or simply went to waste. Albert immediately set about rationalizing this situation. By streamlining and synchronizing the work and staff of the Lord Chamberlain's and Lord Steward's departments into a new department headed by a Master of the Household, a saving of £25,000 was produced in the first year.

Nearly four decades after Albert's death, in 1898, the young apprentice Tschumi was overawed by his first glimpse of the fourteenth-century kitchens at Windsor Castle, comparing them to a chapel 'with its high domed ceiling'. A servant in Queen Victoria's household described them as 'Blunderbore's

146. The Christmas pie with the flaming boar's head is carried in procession for the royal family's meal at Windsor in 1857.

kitchen in a Drury Lane pantomime, where oxen are roasted whole and poor mortals are spitted like larks … quite the most imposing and unique department in the Castle'. More than 100 brightly burnished copper pans on the walls 'blaze like a million suns through a sulphurous London fog'. There was a heated steel dishing-up table, with hollow legs and bottom that filled with steam, 'a good deal larger than the gardens of many suburban houses … and … six meat chopping blocks, each as big as a good-sized dining table'. Against the

white-tiled walls of the double-height kitchen were enormous ovens, roasting ranges, and charcoal and gas stoves. At a desk at one end of the kitchen sat the Clerk of the Kitchen, keeping up to date the kitchen accounts and the bills of fare for each table in the royal household. The chef had his own comfortable room on the north side of the kitchen, to which he could retire – if he ever had the time. The kitchens were a whirlwind of ordered activity. Cooks worked with silent concentration amid the hissing ovens and creaking spits as the

147. The Reform Club kitchen was of the latest design, and attracted cooks from the royal kitchens, such as Charles Francatelli and Alexis Soyer. The latter created a Coronation dish, Lamb Cutlets Reform, still served at the club today. He also designed and ran soup and army kitchens.

clock relentlessly ticked the minutes down to the time the meal must be ready for the royal table (fig. 145).

Cooks and other kitchen staff travelled with the queen and royal household from Buckingham Palace to Windsor, and a small delegation attended them at Osborne and Balmoral. Tschumi was not part of the band chosen to cook at the holiday homes, and so, to gain new experience, he helped out during the royal absences in one of the kitchens in the plethora of new clubs, hotels and restaurants that were springing up in London's West End. Some of the queen's cooks forsook the royal kitchens altogether and rose to become stars of these influential establishments (fig. 147).

148. Queen Victoria had a sweet tooth and loved puddings. Her famous chef Francatelli created for her an imaginative array of puddings, one of which he named 'iced pudding à la Victoria'.

A few, such as Alexis Soyer, who had cooked for the Duke of Cambridge, even interested themselves in how the poor could prepare and cook their daily food, 'so as to obtain from it the greatest amount of nourishment at the least possible expense' (Charles Elmé Francatelli, *A Plain Cookery Book for the Working Classes*, 1852).

Following her long period of withdrawal from public life after Albert's death, many of Queen Victoria's meals were taken with one or two members of her family and her long-

suffering ladies-in-waiting. The queen insisted on punctuality. She also demanded that rooms were regulated to a temperature most people thought cold, with open windows even on chilly days. In addition, a large block of ice was placed in the centre of the dining table. Yet still, on a good day (especially in the privacy of Balmoral), over 'a big tea' or what one of her ladies referred to as 'ladies' dinners', the queen could be very entertaining, 'giving her opinion in a most decided and amusing manner' and often roaring with laughter. Her mimicry was described by a lady-in-waiting as 'too killing!!'

Balmoral was not the favourite venue of most of the household; there, the monotony of boiled beef on Thursdays, pineapple pudding on Fridays – even, as lady-in-waiting Marie Mallet reported, 'the same plum cake, even the number of biscuits on the plate and their variety' – became overwhelmingly tedious (fig. 149). For Queen Victoria, however, its attraction lay in her outings with John Brown, her long-standing ghillie, on whom she became increasingly dependent. When a maid of honour asked Brown if the hamper he was packing into the queen's carriage contained their tea, he replied, 'She don't much like tea – we tak' oot biscuits and sperruts' (fig. 150). Their relationship became a close friendship. He gave her two silver salt cellars in the form of a shell supported by a mermaid, which she

dressed in blue uniforms, stood behind the queen at breakfast, and at dinner dressed in scarlet and gold in winter and white in summer. They slaughtered their own sheep and poultry, and ground Indian spices between flat stones for the curries they cooked daily for the royal table. Karim soon felt that waiting at table was beneath him, and became the queen's Indian Secretary, generally known as the Munshi, teaching the queen Hindustani as a sideline.

Since Albert's death the queen had made several journeys to continental Europe, and

Above: 149. 'Big teas' at Balmoral consisted of tablet, pralines, chocolate sponges, biscuits of many kinds including fondants and wafers, rice cakes and sponge or princess cakes. A different tea service was used for every day of the week.

kept beside her on her lunch table every Sunday for the rest of her life, and she dolefully mourned his death in 1883.

Queen Victoria had found Brown's great devotion to her 'a real comfort'. An unexpected replacement of a kind arrived in the queen's Golden Jubilee year in the form of two Indian servants, one of whom was to hold a prominent role during her remaining years. He was a young man of twenty-four called Abdul Karim. The Indian servants, splendidly

159

151. Queen Victoria, Princess Victoria, Princess Beatrice and the queen's Indian attendants take tea outdoors at Nice in January 1895.

from 1891 she enjoyed a yearly spring holiday in the south of France (figs. 151 and 152). In 1895 she discovered Cimiez, Nice, with its wide boulevard swinging round and up the hill overlooking the bay. She came back every year, and stayed at the Hotel Regina, which had been specially built for her; a marble statue of her was even erected on the boulevard. The queen travelled by train in her own coach with a large bath of ice to reduce the temperature. Hampers were provided for meals en route, including for the ladies-in-waiting every kind of cold meat, stuffed rolls, grouse, 'enough cake and biscuits to set up a baker's shop' (as one lady reported), bottles of hot tea, cream claret, sherry, seltzer water and champagne. The queen's meals in France may have been a melange of English and French cuisines, as a menu sent home by one of her ladies indicates: 'Risotto à la milanaise, grilled mutton chops, poulets aux nouilles, asperges à la sauce, tapioca pudding and meringues aux fraises.'

The queen herself still went on her little adventures, and was spotted with her oldest friend, Lady Jane Churchill, limping along a beach with a donkey and a bath chair. She retained her romantic notion of indigenous foods, and was not averse to sampling the local fare. Many years later, an old Provençal fisherman remembered a strange blue-eyed lady in a purple bonnet landing on the shore. His family invited her into their cave, where they all shared a large pot of bouillabaisse.

Back at home, the queen, now well into her seventies, still insisted on regimenting her own family and household. Every morning at breakfast time, the Clerk of the Kitchen brought up a list of dishes on which the queen, in violet ink, marked up her selection for herself and her family, which now often included her great-grandchildren (fig. 154). Victoria's choice for herself might include brown Windsor soup or white soup, plain roasts (never eaten cold) and a sorbet halfway through the meal, followed by savouries and sweet puddings. Her doctor, Sir James Reid, had prescribed Benger's Food, a powder recommended for children and invalids, as a substitute for other foods, to soothe her colic and indigestion. 'If she would follow a diet and live on Benger's Food and chicken all would be well ... but she clings to roast beef and ices,' claimed one lady in waiting. Not that Victoria disliked the Benger's Food, however; to her doctor's horror, 'instead of substituting it for other foods she adds it to her already copious meals'.

The Aga Khan recalled dining with the queen, when the food kept arriving 'course after course, three or four choices of meat, a hot pudding and an iced pudding, a savoury and all kinds of hothouse fruit ... The queen, in spite of her age, ate and drank heartily – every kind of wine that was offered and every course, including both hot and cold pudding'. The cup that cheered most was still that introduced to her by John Brown – Scotch

153. The menu for Queen Victoria's final Christmas Day, which she spent at Osborne House. The queen died a month later, early in 1901.

OSBORNE

Her Majesty's Dinner.

Christmas Day, 1900

Potages.
Tortue claire   Crême d'orge à l'Américaine

Poissons.
Turbot sauce mousseuse
Filets de sole panés sauce Ravigote

Entrée.
Celestines à la Noël

Relevés.
Dindonneau à la Chipolata
Chine of Pork
Roast Beef   Plum Pudding

Entremets.
Asperges sauce Hollandaise
Mince Pies
Eclairs au chocolat

Buffet
Baron of Beef   Woodcock Pie   Game Pie
Boar's Head   Brawn

154. 'Four Generations': Queen Victoria with her eldest son, Edward, Prince of Wales (later Edward VII), his son George (later George V) and his son David (later Edward VIII) in 1899. David, her great-grandson, was often invited to breakfast or tea with his 'Gangan' Victoria.

whisky – which she had specially distilled for her by John Begg, owner of the new Lochnagar distillery, and which she drank with Apollinaris, soda or Lithia water.

Victoria's breakfasts now usually consisted only of a boiled egg (from Dorking, Surrey) eaten with a gold spoon from a gold egg cup. Her great-grandson David (later Edward VIII) remembered seeing 'Gangan' eating her breakfast in the garden in a little open hut, which could be turned away from the wind. Towards the very end of her life, the queen used a small silver soup basin, kept only for times of illness. It travelled with her to Osborne, but never to Balmoral. It must in some comforting way have reminded her of the little silver bowl she had used as a child at Kensington Palace for her bread and milk; in fact, it may even have been that very bowl.

The queen invited the family as usual for Christmas at Osborne House in 1900, although she felt unequal to joining the celebratory meals (fig. 153). In the early hours of Christmas Day, Lady Jane Churchill died, and within a month Queen Victoria too lay dead at Osborne.

Bertie's Breakfast

'Apple tart without the cheese
Is like a kiss without the squeeze.'

Early twentieth-century rhyme

155. Detail from a painting of 1893 by Pierre-Georges Jeanniot depicting the type of informal tea party the Prince of Wales so much enjoyed; see fig. 163.

The coronation of Edward VII (1901–10) was due to take place on Thursday 26 June 1902. Crowned heads and statesmen of Europe and the world were gathering in London, and a superb banquet for 250 carefully selected guests was being prepared at Buckingham Palace, exercising to the full the very considerable skills of the exacting Monsieur Ménager and his team of cooks in the royal kitchens. A fourteen-course banquet incorporating the most exquisite dishes had been worked out in close collaboration with the new king. It was to begin with *consommé de faisan aux quenelles,* followed by *côtelettes de bécassines à la Souvaroff* and ending with *caisses de fraises Miramare* – each an inordinately time-consuming dish to prepare. The consommé was to be garnished with quenelles of forcemeat, coloured red, white and green; for the Souvaroff dish it was necessary to bone 250 snipe before making the cutlets, which were then stuffed with foie gras before being placed in a pig's caul to cook; and the cases for the strawberry dessert were shaped individually from spun sugar and filled with a delicious strawberry and liqueur jelly, containers of which now covered every kitchen surface. Some 2500 quails, 300 legs of mutton and 80 chickens, and quantities of Russian caviar, sturgeon, truffles, mushrooms, asparagus and strawberries, began the list of orders. There had been difficulty with some of the deliveries and it was discovered late

164

156. The coronation banquet of George III and Queen Charlotte in Westminster Hall, 1761. A banquet on this scale was never envisaged for the coronation of Edward VII, but a very special meal was prepared for the 250 kings and heads of state who had been invited.

157. The Exeter Salt, a silver-gilt turreted castle studded with emeralds, amethysts and garnets, was presented to Charles II as a gift of allegiance from the City of Exeter on his restoration to the throne in 1660. More commonly known as the Salt of State, it has been used at many coronation banquets.

in the day that not enough caviar had been ordered. Now that all the food was safely in the kitchens and the preparation in full swing, the cooks worked cheerfully into the night to get everything ready in time.

On Wednesday 25 June Sir Frederick Treves, the king's doctor, sends for the Master of the Household, Lord Farquhar, who sends for Monsieur Ménager, the Royal Chef, who tells the kitchen staff that the king is seriously ill and will undergo an emergency operation that very evening. The coronation is postponed; what is to happen now?

The greatest feast the royal cooks are ever called on to produce must surely be the coronation banquet. It is the sovereign's first celebratory statement of his changed status as head of the nation and his new standing among the heads of other nations, after the long and solemn ritual of crowning. It affirms the loyalty of his subjects. This last was done quite literally as late as the reign of George IV, with the monarch's champion riding on horseback into the hall during the coronation dinner and throwing down a gauntlet to offer single combat to any person daring to 'deny or gainsay our Sovereign Lord' (fig. 131).

The coronation banquet was traditionally held in Westminster Hall, with the newly crowned sovereign and peers processing across the road from Westminster Abbey. Henry IV's feast on 13 October 1399 was made up of only three courses, but each of these consisted of at least twelve dishes, including sturgeon, gilded chickens, peacocks, cranes and bitterns. Almost 300 years later, on the dais in Westminster Hall, joint monarchs William (1689–1702) and Mary (1689–94) took their seats at the royal table. Those not lucky enough to be invited to the coronation banquet itself let down improvised baskets and napkins from the makeshift galleries above, in the hope of hoisting back a little sustenance. William IV (1830–37) was of the opinion that coronation was a costly charade. He insisted that, like Napoleon, he

158. Gabriel Tschumi joined the royal kitchens at the age of sixteen in the last years of Queen Victoria's reign, and worked under Monsieur Ménager to prepare the coronation meal for Edward VII. He continued to cook for the royal family for more than forty years.

was perfectly capable of crowning himself, but he eventually succumbed to a cheap 'half crownation' with no banquet. The nineteen-year-old Victoria at the end of her coronation day had sat down to dinner with the family ('we thirteen') and her prime minister, Lord Melbourne. There were fireworks in Hyde Park for her to watch before bedtime from the balcony at Buckingham Palace (fig. 159).

Victoria's eldest son, Albert Edward, Prince of Wales, was fifty-nine when he finally came to the throne, and had a reputation as a bon viveur. In the summer of 1902, amid the building pressure as coronation day approached, it was observed that the king was eating too much. He had developed pains in his lower abdomen, but he ignored them, feeling impelled to carry on with the preparations for this great event. When his doctors told him the

coronation must be postponed, he ordered them to leave the room. He declared that he would go to his coronation even if he were to drop dead during the service, but in the event he developed peritonitis. His doctors warned him that without an operation he would certainly drop dead before he even got to Westminster Abbey, and an operating theatre

159. In 1838 the citizens of Cambridge celebrated Queen Victoria's coronation in great style, with a dinner held for 15,000 people on Parker's Piece.

160. Some 500,000 of London's poor were invited to dinner at the king's expense in July 1902 to celebrate his coronation. It was reported that the tents in one of the venues, Bishop's Park in Fulham, covered an area of 2½ square miles and provided 5 miles of seating.

was prepared inside Buckingham Palace. In 1902 a surgical procedure of this kind was not without risk for a heavily smoking 16-stone man in his sixtieth year. Sir Frederick Treves, was, however, a most capable surgeon; one of his other patients was Joseph Merrick, better known as the Elephant Man. The operation on the king was successfully completed in less than an hour, and by the following morning – which should have been that of his coronation – he was sitting up in bed, puffing on one of his favourite cigars.

Meanwhile, down in the palace kitchens, panic mingled with growing despair as the exhausted cooks stared at row upon row of ingredients (fig. 158). Every conceivable vessel was filled with liqueur jelly, and the sheer volume of food meant that the kitchens were literally out of action. The Clerk of the Kitchen, who had wrongly ordered only half the quantity of caviar from Russia (now a blessing in disguise), had the bright idea of melting down the jellies and storing them in magnum champagne bottles until they were required, when the bottles could be warmed and the jellies poured into their cases. The quails were put into the cold store and the caviar into boxes of ice, but there was no way of storing the large quantities of cooked chicken, partridge, sturgeon, snipe, fruit and cream. The kitchen staff themselves may have sampled the dishes, but they can have had little appetite. It was decided, therefore, to offer the food to the Little Sisters of the Poor to distribute to the hungry and homeless of the East End of London. It was to be a discreet handover, and the cooks would never know what was thought of their two long weeks of dedicated work. The East Enders must have been puzzled at food the like of which they had never tasted, and one wonders whether they enjoyed it. Probably they would have preferred a plain dinner of roast beef – but that was also on offer in the summer of 1902.

Holborn, Finsbury and Shoreditch. The dinners in Shoreditch, which catered for 15,000 people, took place in a variety of halls; some were even delivered to the guests' own homes. The fare served in that part of the city was typical: roast beef, pork, ham, potatoes, hot plum pudding, preserved fruit, jam roll, bread and cheese, pickles, aerated water, lime juice and cider. Some 18,000 packets of tobacco and cigarettes were donated by Imperial Tobacco, boxes of chocolates were supplied courtesy of Messrs Rowntree of York, and there were also gifts of portraits of the king and queen. During the day, the Prince and Princess of Wales and other members of the royal family, in place of the king and queen, made a tour in open carriages to the diners in all these deprived areas of London, bringing the king's good wishes and reporting on his improving health. They were greeted with loud cheers and the singing of the national anthem.

Meanwhile the king convalesced on his yacht, on a diet of chicken mousse and boiled fish, building up his health and strength for his actual coronation, which finally took place on 9 August. Some of the overseas delegations had by this time returned to their own countries. For the remainder of the guests, the royal cooks duly prepared the over-hung quail, extracted the liqueur jelly from the champagne bottles and served up the same menu. The table was decorated with sugar

161. In a painting of 1902 by William Hatherell, Edward VII gives an after-dinner speech to family and friends on board HMS *Ophir*, shortly after his accession in 1901. Every August the king joined the festivities on his yacht during Cowes Week.

'The King's Dinner to the Poor' – a celebratory coronation dinner and festivities for 'the submerged tenth,' London's poor – took place on Saturday 5 July 1902 (fig. 160). The weather was charming, the arrangements excellent, the help abundant and the populace delighted. Dinners were offered across the capital, in Paddington, Fulham, Poplar, Hackney, Stepney, Marylebone, St Pancras, ribbons and flowers, and a large sugar plaque was made bearing the royal crest. With their *caisses de fraises Miramare* – which were a great success – the guests each received a small sugar crown as a memento of the dinner. For the cooks below stairs, no such reminder of this time was required; nor would they have the opportunity ever again to produce a coronation banquet of this extravagance.

Albert Edward was called Bertie not as an abbreviation of affection but to distinguish him from his father, the divine Albert, whom his mother hoped Bertie would in time come

to replicate as closely as was humanly possible. Instantly failing to live up to this Olympian ideal, the poor boy was condemned by Albert as 'unsatisfactory' and 'a cunning lazybones' and crammed with lessons, morals and reminders of his duties, so that – unsurprisingly – he developed into the opposite of his aesthetic, work-driven, depressed, unsociable father. 'Poor Bertie' became an epicurean with a huge appetite for food, clothes, society, women and sport. On his fifteenth birthday he was already overweight, and it was suggested that he

162. In November 1903 Edward VII held a state banquet for Victor Emmanuel III and Queen Elena of Italy in St George's Hall, Windsor. In some measure, this banquet must have cheered the royal cooks after their disappointment at the coronation dinner.

163. From a painting by Pierre-Georges Jeanniot, 1893. Teatime was the Edwardian time of day to relax and unbend – literally, since the ladies removed their constricting whalebone corsets.

go on a diet, choosing his own food 'in accordance with what the physicians say is good for you', as his mother put it in a letter. This proving a complete failure, he was prescribed a diet of bread, butter and an egg with tea, coffee or cocoa for breakfast; a light luncheon of meat and vegetables without pudding and with only seltzer water to drink; more of the same for dinner; and a cup of tea before bed. Nothing was more likely to turn a fifteen-year-old's fertile and febrile fantasies into future food surfeits. He was an overeater in the making. However, he never

just ate; he ate because he loved food and cared very much about what he consumed. The only problem was that he invariably ate too much.

Bertie's breakfast, when he grew up and regained control of his diet, would include bacon, eggs, haddock, kippers, chicken, cutlets, porridge, toast and butter. A breakfast served to him (now Edward VII) and his queen, Alexandra, on 11 February 1904 at Windsor Castle listed on its menu:

Petites sole frits

Haddock à l'anglaise

Œufs en cocotte

Bacon à l'anglaise

Poulets grillés à la diable

Bécassines sur canapés

Les viandes froides à la gelée

A flask of hot turtle soup would be prepared should Bertie be peckish during the morning. Luncheon, at 2.30 pm, was hearty but always elegant. A typical luncheon prepared at Ascot for Bertie and his party in June 1908 went as follows:

Consommé froid

Mousse de crabe, sauce rémoulade
Filets de saumon à l'Isabelle
Chaufroix de volaille à la Valenciennes
Jambonneaux à la Montranchez
Cailles froides à la Bohémienne

Asperges en branches froides

Eton mess aux cerises
*Gooseberry fool * Pâtisseries à la Parisienne*
Biscuits glacés aux pêches
Mignardises

Dessert

BUFFET
Derby beef
Agneau, sauce menthe

*Bœuf roti * Bœuf presse*
*Galantine de volaille * Langue à l'écarlate*
*Jambon d'York * Pâté de poulets*
Poulets à la gelée

Salade de Romaine

*Gateaux de pain bis * Tarte de groseilles*
Babas aux liqueurs

Tea was always served for the prince, and later for the king, at 5 pm in whatever house he happened to find himself. As ladies were never invited to a luncheon served in one of the newfangled restaurants, they would happily change into a fashionable tea gown and join the gentlemen for rolls, sandwiches, cold meat, scones, hot cakes, cold cakes, shortcake, petits fours, macaroons and crumpets. The loosely fastened tea gown enabled them to remove their tightly laced stays and relax with the gentlemen of their choice for 'le five o'clock' in whichever way they preferred (Bertie preferring both tea and lady whenever available) (fig. 163).

By 8.30 pm the men would need to be dressed in the short black 'dinner' jacket newly invented by Bertie, or in full evening dress if dining at the palace. The ladies, laced back into their corsets, were required to appear in their tiaras and evening gowns, scented, serene and quite recovered from tea, ready for a twelve-course dinner (fig. 165). This might start with a light consommé and progress to fish served

164. Queen Alexandra had a very small appetite and remained slim all her life. She was appalled at her husband's overeating.

165. The Dining Room at Sandringham in the late nineteenth century. Queen Victoria disapproved of many of her eldest son's friends who were invited to stay there at this time.

with sauce or poached in Chablis; seafood (oysters were especially popular); game of all kinds in season, stuffed with truffles and foie gras; roast meat; chicken and turkey in aspic; asparagus; cheese soufflé; and desserts of fruit dressed with liqueur and cream. Bertie also loved plain dishes, as long as they were well cooked. Roast beef with Yorkshire pudding was on the menu every Sunday at Sandringham, and at Balmoral there was Scotch broth, Irish stew and plum pudding with a weekly dose of haggis. Almost the only food the king spurned was starchy dishes, such as macaroni.

Supper consisted of cold meat with sandwiches, cakes and cheese, although the king was partial to grilled oysters for his own meal. At the end of the day, with a tray of cold chicken in his bedroom in case of need during

the night, he would light his twelfth cigar or perhaps his twentieth Egyptian cigarette of the day and breathe a sigh – or a burp – of repletion.

Alexandra, Bertie's svelte Danish wife, was to tell his doctors that the amount of food her husband got through was 'terrible', and beyond anything she had ever seen. She herself had but a small appetite (fig. 164). She might have an *œuf en cocotte* for breakfast or even a little cold meat in jelly, pick at lunch, possibly skip tea, nearly always be late for dinner and, in the evening, order a tray of sandwiches and cold chicken to be left outside her room. It was eventually discovered that the sandwiches were almost certainly for her beloved dogs. The king's wire-haired terrier, Caesar, was more straightforward; he came directly to the kitchen and was given titbits or a bone for his efforts.

Bertie's appetites had been cultivated and sharpened not only in London's aristocratic circles but also in the world at large. He had been sent in his teenage years on study tours to Germany, Switzerland, France and Italy by his father, Albert, in the hope that he would acquire a grasp of European art, history and literature. Instead, to Albert's horror, Bertie discovered new fashions, his first girl to kiss and new foods to enjoy. He also charmed most of the people he met, including the painter Frederic Leighton and the writers Edward Lear and Robert Browning. He gave a dinner in Rome for the last, who described him as a gentle, refined boy. Browning obviously failed to inculcate a lifetime love of literature in his host, however: later in life, the king, presenting a prize for a book on Lamb, imagined it to be an eccentric cookery tome. He had already had someone from the upmarket bookshop Hatchards come to Sandringham to fill his bookshelves by the yard with whatever they deemed suitable for that kind of house. By this time it was accepted that Bertie preferred good food to mental effort.

167. Edward VII, as Prince of Wales, stands over a wild Chillingham bull he shot during a visit to Chillingham Castle, Northumberland, in 1879.

168. After the bag of pheasants was examined (seen here in about 1905), Edward VII's shooting party at Sandringham would be joined by the ladies for a hot buffet in a tent heated by a stove – much needed in the freezing midwinters of Norfolk.

In 1860, aged nineteen, Bertie had been sent on his first overseas visit as a representative of the royal family, to Canada and the United States. People loved him, and he seemed to like them. His face became well known, and appeared on advertisements for cider and on such items as tins of beans and pork. He attended banquets and discovered new dishes. Perhaps one of the few occasions when he did not like the food he saw was at a fair in St Louis, where sides of beef and buffalo were hacked at with pocket knives in the saloon bar by men simultaneously spewing into spittoons.

In 1869 Bertie and Alexandra, their four children and their household sailed down the Nile followed by a barge containing their provisions, including 3000 bottles of champagne and 4000 of claret. They brought

back from the trip a ten-year-old Nubian orphan who, always dressed in his native clothing, served coffee at Sandringham. In 1875–76 the Prince of Wales made a hugely successful state visit to India. He took with him in his entourage three cooks, but returned with an Indian chef from Madras to make curry for him.

Interesting though these trips had been, it was time and time again to France that Bertie returned for its food, its women, its fashion and its ambience, and it was here that he felt most at home. His trips took him from Paris, with its gaiety girls who called out to him for champagne from the stage of the Moulin Rouge, to Biarritz and Monte Carlo, where the chef Auguste Escoffier concocted mouth-watering dishes for him, stunningly presented (fig. 166).

169. Frank Watkins, *Study of the Interior of the Kitchen at Windsor Castle with a Visit by the Royal Family*, 1886. The image possibly depicts Princess Alexandra in the foreground, discussing the week's royal menus or a special dinner with her cooks. Each of the copper pans was numbered so that, after use, the scullery maid could return it to its rightful position.

All these experiences were taken back to London and melded into the kind of cuisine that Bertie enjoyed. Menus at the royal palaces had been French-influenced virtually since the Middle Ages, but after Charles II's indulgences and George IV's overblown affair with Antonin Carême's cooking, Edward VII was the first king truly to appreciate the subtleties of classic French cuisine. He liaised regularly with his cooks, but, even so, they resorted on occasion to bribing a footman to hear what his reaction to certain dishes had been. The king, it would appear, enjoyed everything that was served to him.

The king's food patterns revolved around the fixed routine of his year. In November the royal family went to Sandringham to celebrate the king's birthday on the 9th and Queen Alexandra's on 1 December. They stayed on for Christmas and shooting parties (fig. 168). Each year, 'dear sweet' Alexandra was presented by the kitchen staff with a huge and carefully decorated birthday cake, about one-third of her

170. Edward, Prince of Wales ('Bertie') by Alexander Bassano, *c.* 1871. Bertie had got himself into so many scrapes by 1871 that Sir Henry Ponsonby complained that 'London was black with the smoke of burning confidential letters'.

171. During the 1880s César Ritz and Auguste Escoffier ran the Grand Hôtel in Monte Carlo, where they provided comfort and exquisite food for the Prince of Wales. Escoffier later ran the Savoy and Carlton restaurants in London; Ritz gave his name to new hotels in Paris and London.

own weight. On one occasion it was decorated with roses, violets, carnations and pansies made with such care that those present took them to be real flowers. At Christmas, royal servants and workers on the estate were given small presents from the tree, and each family received a joint of beef. Additionally, they were entitled to a twice-yearly brace of pheasants and a haunch of venison.

In February it was off to France, to the spring of the Riviera and Nice's spring festival Bataille des Fleurs. One of the meals prepared during the 1880s for Bertie by Escoffier, head chef at the Grand Hôtel in Monte Carlo (fig. 171), went as follows:

Caviar frais

Velouté d'écrevisse au beurre d'Isigny

Nosteles à l'anglaise

Selle d'agneau de lait de Pauillac

Petit pois frais du pays

Pomme de terre Rosette

Perdreaux cocotte Périgourdine

Salade de laitues rouges

Cœurs d'artichaux à la moelle et parmesan

Mousse à la vanille accompagnée de cerises jubilées

Friandise de Monte Carlo

Café mode Turque

Grande fine champagne 1860

Chartreuse de couvent

Champagne brut lafite 1874

Porto vieux

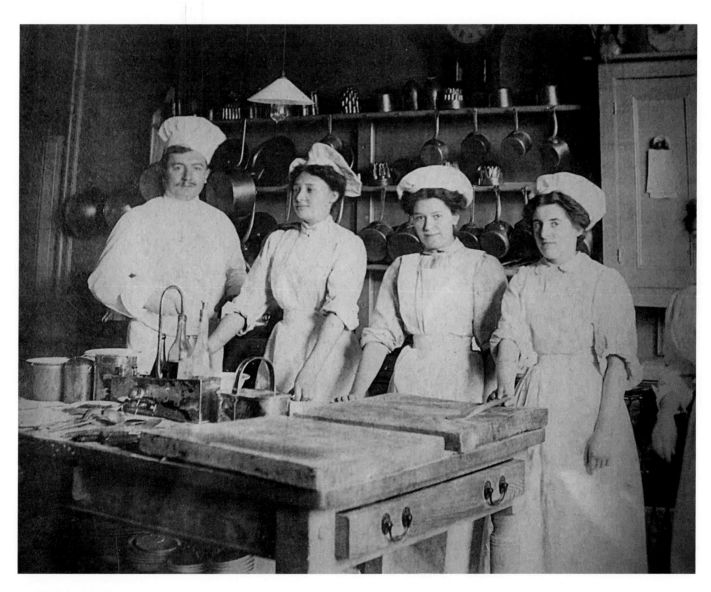

172. Monsieur Delachaume
and his staff in the kitchens
at Polesden Lacey, Surrey,
c. 1905. The socialite Margaret
Greville invited Edward VII
to a house party there in
June 1909. Her chef invented
dishes for the occasion,
including iced saddle of
lamb, Moscow style, and
quails with ortolans.

173. Organized by Mary Hooper, the author of numerous cookery books, the Young Ladies' School of Cooking opened in 1880 and held courses at Crystal Palace and South Kensington, teaching basic cookery skills to ladies, not servants.

174. Edward, Prince of Wales and other guests at a house party at Mar Lodge in the Highlands. Wherever he was, the prince liked to have fun.

Bertie usually visited Paris on his own, and stayed at the Ritz or the Bristol. He shopped, went to the theatre and dined in clubs, some of doubtful repute, with ladies of a similar character. On one occasion he was enticed to play the part of a murdered prince in a play starring Sarah Bernhardt, after which he took her for dinner in a private room at the Café Anglais.

In later years, the king stayed at Biarritz at the same time as his mistress, Alice Keppel, and her two daughters. Sonia Keppel remembered seeing 'Kingy', as she called him, every day. They had picnics on tables with linen tablecloths and silver and 'every variety of cold

food'. The king pretended anonymity, but – very like his mother before him – was irritated if he was not instantly recognized and given due reverence. When they lunched in the hotel it was in a private dining room with a sea view, from a menu of plovers' eggs, trout or salmon, lamb or chicken, asparagus and strawberries. Before he returned home, there was usually a short cruise on the Mediterranean with Alexandra and the children.

Back in England, it was straight into the London Season, with balls, garden parties, dinner parties, opera, theatre and racing. At Covent Garden, the royal cook would bring a ten-course meal to be served in the king's box on gold and silver plate during the interval. Then there would be hampers for the Derby at Epsom, where turtle soup and whitebait were popular dishes, followed in June by Royal Ascot, which was always smarter and usually included a pigeon pie in the ten-course picnic. In August, Cowes Week was spent on the yacht, with local shrimps and lobsters on the menu.

Most years, in August, Bertie would take a trip to the spa resorts of Baden-Baden or Marienbad, where he drank the waters and – 'pour combattre l'obésité' – attempted a diet of simple fare, such as local fish, game and peaches. He sometimes lost as much as 8 lb in his fortnight there. In October he would go to Scotland with a party to hunt stags. Such warming soups as mulligatawny were served, as well as hashed venison and game pie. Haggis was on the menu, but it was not a dish enjoyed by either Bertie or Alexandra.

Whether at Buckingham Palace, Sandringham, Balmoral or Windsor, or at a restaurant in London, Paris or Monte Carlo, dinner with Bertie was fun (fig. 174). People enjoyed themselves, even though, as had his mother, he insisted on guests being on time and ate at a good pace. Unlike his mother, however, he was a good listener and positively enjoyed his guests' company. As a grown man,

Bertie had once been found hiding behind a pillar trembling, afraid to go in to dinner with his mother because he was late. He, on the contrary, fitted in with his guests when necessary. When an Indian prince dining at Buckingham Palace surprised everyone by throwing asparagus stalks over his shoulder, the king followed suit, and then so did everyone else. The queen could even take jokes that involved her own discomfort. When the royal party was dining on the train en route to Berlin, the footman lost his balance as the train suddenly stopped, cascading a dish of quails over her head. 'I shall arrive *coiffée de cailles*', she quipped. The king was less good at jokes at his own expense, although he was not averse to offering his friends what he could not take: on the odd occasion, filling mince-pie cases with mustard or placing lobsters in his guests' beds.

Bertie loved having children around at mealtimes, although his mother had commanded that her grandchildren were not to mix with her son's 'fast friends' and that they were to eat in a separate room. Fast friends, fast cars and fast women were all part of Bertie's life, and so were children. His grandson David (the future Edward VIII, 1936) once interrupted him when he was eating, but was told to let the king finish speaking. He did, although it was then too late to tell his grandfather that there was a slug on his lettuce, which by that time he had eaten. In Biarritz, Sonia Keppel remembered placing penny bets with the king on which pieces of bread, butter-side down, would slide fastest down the stripes of his trouser leg. Combined with his popularity, his sociable dinners gave Bertie, both as Prince of Wales and, more importantly, as king, the opportunity to conduct discreet diplomacy in a way that would have been totally foreign to his parents, who preferred to write interminable memos rather than indulge in conversation.

Gabriel Tschumi remembered a song the kitchen staff used to sing, which (he thought) went something like this: 'So long as there's a king like good King Edward, there'll be no war.' But when the king died in May 1910, an end soon came to peace and to the Edwardian days of plenty. In a few years, austerity and ration books would be on the menu for discussion among the cooks in the royal kitchens.

176. A caricature of
Edward, Prince of Wales
surrounded by the
courtesans of Paris, *c.* 1900.
'Edward the Caresser'
visited Paris *en garçon*,
enjoying himself as a
player in la belle époque.
He strolled the Champs-
Elysées, met beautiful
women, drank the finest
wines and dined in style.
Soufflé à la Marigny at the
Café Anglais, he declared,
was even better than his
own cook could make.

Dessin de Roubille

The End of Conspicuous Consumption

'Manger est un besoin; mais savoir manger est un art.'
('To eat is a requirement; to know how to eat is an art.')

François de La Rochefoucauld

177. Sir James Gunn, *Conversation Piece at the Royal Lodge, Windsor*, 1950. King George VI, Queen Elizabeth and princesses Elizabeth and Margaret take tea together.

For centuries it had been the custom that the rich, the aristocracy or those aspiring to either copied sovereign and court in their dress, furnishings and, above all, food. The banquet – banqueting food originally meaning a sweetmeat following a feast – was uniquely the province of royalty. The variety of food created in the royal kitchens, together with its presentation on silver-gilt dishes, served by liveried footmen in the most sumptuous surroundings, exhibited daily the status and wealth of the monarch (fig. 178).

In the twentieth century, however, in a climate of democracy and under the spotlight of increasingly unblinking media scrutiny, royalty was constantly urged to show itself concerned with common causes. For the first time, food consumed in the palace or on family picnics was required to be seen in a new light as 'normal' food. In dress, too, king or queen and court no longer dictated the fashion. By the end of the century, the universal jeans were worn by younger members of the royal family for informal occasions, as they were by 95 per cent of their peers. Such social pressure towards homogeneity occasionally resulted in popular role-playing for amusement, where the masses flocked to 'Tudor' royal banquets or paid to have their wedding breakfast in a castle or enjoy an exclusive Georgian dinner in a palace (fig. 179).

Although Edward VII had been a gourmet, his son George V (1910–36), who had spent

178. At a State Banquet for the Amir of Kuwait at Windsor Castle in November 2012, the guests dined on poached turbot, Windsor partridge and dark chocolate gateau.

many years in the navy, had grown accustomed to its cooking. On his accession, without any prompting, he personally found that it was all he required or wanted. His wife, however, relished classic French cuisine, and she regulated to a large extent the meals served in the royal palaces, reviving many standard dishes of Edwardian times. George V might have preferred Irish stew, shepherd's pie and cutlets, and mashed potato with everything; Queen Mary insisted on variation and fancy menus even for her tea parties, at which the

179. A table is set out for a Georgian dinner at Kew Palace, 2011. The intimate settings for these eighteenth-century-style dinners have made them very popular.

180. George V (seated front left) has lunch during a tiger shoot in India in 1911.

cakes were given English names but the sandwiches curiously labelled with such titles as *bridge rolls aux œufs et cresson* and *sandwiches saumon fumé*.

Despite the queen's exacting standards, some dietary drabness took hold of court and country, owing in large measure to the rationing of most basic foodstuffs during and following the two world wars. Even food for the royal family was dictated by the number of coupons in their personal ration books (fig. 182). The consequences of this are shown most starkly in the wedding breakfast of Princess Elizabeth and Philip, Duke of Edinburgh in November 1947 (fig. 183). The menu consisted of only three courses, and one of the royal chefs estimated that it lasted only twenty minutes:

181. In a very rare picture of Queen Mary, she is seen informally eating an apple with her daughter Mary and a companion at Sandringham in 1911.

182. Queen Mary's wartime food ration book, 1944–45. Even members of the royal family were issued with ration books, and given the same allowances as everyone else, both during and after the war.

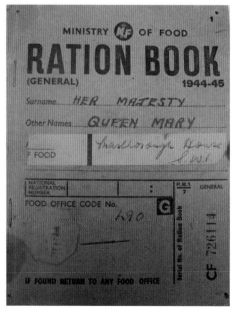

Filet de Sole Mountbatten

———

Perdreau en Casserole
*Haricots Verts * Pommes Noisette*
Salade Royale

———

Bombe Glacée Princesse Elizabeth
Friandises [petits fours]

———

Déssert

———

Café

Compared to one of Edward VII's dinners, it was merely a snack; compared to a royal everyday pre-war dinner, it was very plain

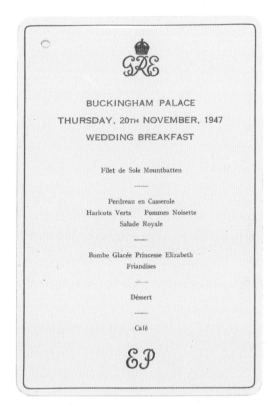

183. Menu for the wedding breakfast of Princess Elizabeth and Philip, Duke of Edinburgh at Buckingham Palace, 20 November 1947.

184. Princess Elizabeth's wedding cake was made in a time of austerity by McVitie & Price. Because of a shortage of raisins and currants in Britain, a supply was sent by Girl Guides in Australia.

immediate family and the heads of the royal families of Greece, Romania, Norway and Denmark. In the background, a medley of popular music was played by the string band of the Grenadier Guards. The meal ended traditionally, with the cutting of the wedding cake. Despite the acute shortages of dried fruit, many firms wrote to offer their cake-making services (fig. 184).

Although sugar was available only on ration coupons until September 1953, food

indeed. The bombe glacée, named after the princess, harks back to the grand puddings of the Victorian era and Francatelli's famous iced bombe, which he named for Queen Victoria (fig. 148). The rest of the meal is commonplace. How royal can a salad be? Partridges were not rationed, so a fish course could be introduced. What is possibly more amazing than the austerity of the meal is the fact that even after two great wars, and with all the nationalism of the twentieth century, the menu is still written completely in French. At least this menu is correct French (apart from the addition of an accent to *dessert*); often the written French relayed from chef to table resulted in an indecipherable menu card of culinary franglais.

More than 100 guests sat down to the wedding breakfast at twenty-six tables in Buckingham Palace. The bride and groom sat at a table of ten, composed of the bride's

gradually became more plentiful, and when the time came the country was looking forward to a June coronation with street parties and celebrations. Coronation Chicken was invented by Constance Spry and Rosemary Hume, the principals of the Cordon Bleu Cookery School. It was a stroke of genius combining three great loves of the British people – curry, chicken and mayonnaise – and became a classic dish. It had originally been conceived as Jubilee Chicken for George V in 1935 and, ever popular, it reappears regularly in sandwiches and on picnic menus.

185. Queen Elizabeth The Queen Mother shares her birthday cake with Sir Frederick Ashton at a Royal Ballet party in Covent Garden in 1980.

186. A street party in Chichester Road, Leytonstone, to celebrate the coronation of Queen Elizabeth II in June 1953. In many areas of the United Kingdom, despite chilly weather, streets were decorated with Union Jacks and bunting, and long tables set out for street parties.

corporate manufacturers. A four-day festival at Buckingham Palace in 2013 celebrated the sixtieth anniversary of Elizabeth II's coronation with an exhibition showing a selection of her favourite goods under royal warrant.

The present trend away from over-elaborate royal meals has been reinforced by the strong convictions of the Prince of Wales and the founding of his company, Duchy Originals, in 1990. The Prince wholeheartedly supports the growing of wholesome, sustainable, seasonal and organic food, healthily steering away from the popular profusion of cheap fast foods and low-quality convenience meals. The Duchy logo has

187. An advertisement for the Cycle Biscuit clearly displays the warrant to supply Queen Victoria. The marketing power that an association with the royal family provided for 'branding' products was recognized very early in the history of advertising.

188. An advertisement from the 1920s for a new French dessert. It is nostalgically called 'La Favorite du Roi', there now being no French royal family to endorse it.

The twentieth century saw an unprecedented rise in consumerism and, alongside it, the power of advertising. Royal patronage and the logo of a royal warrant became greatly sought after as an aid to increasing sales (figs. 187 and 188). The royal page-turned-grocer, William Fortnum, had begun to exhibit royal arms on his shop and produce in the eighteenth century, but it was under Queen Victoria that the royal warrant became almost commonplace, with some 2000 being issued. In more recent times, more than ninety have been granted to food suppliers, from local producers to global

189. Prince Charles shares a simple lunch outdoors with his grandmother, Queen Elizabeth The Queen Mother, at Balmoral in the 1980s. The Queen Mother enjoyed eating outdoors, and often took lunch at Clarence House under the large plane trees in her garden, which she named her *salon vert*.

become established as indicating a prestige brand that represents reliable good quality, protection for the environment and sustainable organic production. Its motto 'Is good, does good and tastes good' refers to the fact that part of the proceeds go to support the Prince's charities.

The Queen's eightieth birthday dinner, held at George III's little royal palace at Kew in April 2006, illustrated this tendency to greater awareness and sustainability. The food was seasonal and mainly organic, much of it from the Prince of Wales's estate at Highgrove, Gloucestershire, with venison from Sandringham, and Morecambe Bay shrimps and salmon as a first course. The meal ended naturally with a birthday cake. This menu might have been sourced with imagination and carefully cooked for a special family dinner to celebrate the birthday of any mother or grandmother anywhere in the country (fig. 193).

Alongside the trend and pressure for the royals to behave as 'a family', one must not lose

190. Prince Charles prepares food in his lodgings while a student at Cambridge in 1969.

191. An exhibition at Buckingham Palace in 2008 saw the Ballroom prepared as for a state banquet for 170 guests, with the great horseshoe table laid out with silver-gilt place settings, candelabra and flowers. The Queen inspected the display before it was opened to the public.

sight of the most important role still played by the monarch in state visits and banquets, which are carried out to a standard unequalled anywhere in the world, and which never fail to impress, astonish and amaze all who witness or take part in them (figs. 191 and 192). There have been about 100 state banquets during the present reign, each requiring immaculate planning on many levels and in different spheres. Usually now composed of four courses, they last about

an hour and a half and normally take place at Windsor Castle or Buckingham Palace. The end of the banquet and the summons to coffee and petits fours is still heralded, as in Queen Victoria's day, by a skirl of Scottish pipes.

Following the fairytale wedding of Prince William to Catherine Middleton in April 2011, The Queen held a lunchtime reception for her grandson and his bride in the state rooms at Buckingham Palace, where Prince Charles's

192. The Queen inspects the table in St George's Hall, Windsor, as it is prepared for a state banquet.

193. This is the menu served to The Queen and her family at her eightieth birthday party, which took place in George III's dining room at Kew Palace in 2006. Not only is the food English, but so is the menu too.

Buckingham Palace, where they were served vintage pink champagne and elderflower cocktails before going in to dinner in the ballroom. The 300 guests were seated at thirty round tables decorated with white flowers and candles. As with the canapés served earlier, the theme of the food was local and organic. The menu was put together by the Swiss chef Anton Mosimann, and began with dressed crab, crayfish and prawns from Wales with salmon from a Scottish loch and langoustines from the Hebrides. The main course was fillet

harpist, Claire Jones, played and Pol Roger champagne was served. Some 10,000 canapés had been made by the royal cooks supervised by the Royal Chef, Mark Flanagan: Cornish crab salad on lemon blinis and smoked salmon on beetroot ones, as well as the more usual cheese straws, miniature roast-beef dinners and chipolatas; and chocolate pralines, rhubarb crème brûlée and raspberry tartlets. There was also a special large chocolate-biscuit cake – a favourite with Prince William since his childhood. The climax of the meal was, of course, the wedding cake, created by Fiona Cairns. It was an eight-tier fruit cake – or rather seventeen fruit cakes – iced with white and cream icing and decorated with seventeen different flower designs (fig. 194).

In the evening, bagpipes played more guests into the now candlelit state rooms of

194. Each sugar flower on the wedding cake for Prince William and Catherine Middleton had an allegorical meaning: roses for happiness; lily of the valley for sweetness and humility; daffodils, thistles and shamrocks representing Wales, Scotland and Ireland; and, of course, sweet william.

of Castle of Mey lamb with Highgrove spring vegetables, and the meal ended with a pudding of trifle, chocolate fondant and ice cream in brandy-snap baskets.

Queen Elizabeth's Diamond Jubilee – only the second royal Diamond Jubilee to occur in Britain – was celebrated in June 2012. In a miserably wet summer, it was hardly surprising that a Diamond Jubilee rain poncho formed part of the picnic kits given to 12,000 guests to enjoy in the gardens of Buckingham Palace

on 4 June. The menu for these packs was put together by the celebrated chef Heston Blumenthal and Mark Flanagan. Again, the theme was great British produce and the picnics included seasonal raw vegetables – celery, carrots and red peppers – strawberries from Sandringham, chocolate cake and lemon and caraway Madeira cake. There was a touch of nostalgia, too, in the inclusion of Coronation Chicken (in a new form with sesame seeds, renamed Diamond Jubilee Chicken).

Eight pupils from four schools were selected by competition to create a modern Jubilee menu, and invited to Buckingham Palace to prepare their dishes to serve to The Queen and her guests (fig. 195). Among the imaginative dishes chosen were Luvlee Jublee Bublee, an elderflower, strawberry and champagne soup; Beefeater's Delight, duchess potatoes with horseradish and Gloucester beef; Golden Carriages, filo pastry filled with diced apricots, pistachios and honey; and Diamond Slippers, cake and

195. The Duchess of Cornwall launches a competition for schoolchildren to produce a dish for The Queen's Diamond Jubilee in 2012.

sugar-paste slippers studded with edible 'diamonds'.

A more traditional Jubilee banquet took place in Westminster Hall, where Richard II had celebrated his coronation banquet some 635 years earlier, in 1377 (fig. 196). The Queen was escorted into the hall by her Lord Great Chamberlain, the Marquess of Cholmondeley, to a fanfare of trumpets. The banquet was hosted by the livery companies, and Thomas Sheldon, the Master Mercer, spoke of the age of Elizabeth. He told The Queen: 'You embody the very best of our national values … . You are a constant in a changing world'. The Speaker of the House of Commons said grace.

Instead of sitting alone under a canopy of state, as Richard II had done and any monarch up to the nineteenth century might have been expected to do, The Queen sat at one of the thirty tables, each of which accommodated ten people. The National Children's Orchestra of Great Britain played at the beginning of the meal, which consisted of seasonal British food: Scottish salmon, asparagus from the Isle of Wight, Welsh lamb and Sandringham apple sauce, accompanied by English sparkling wine and Sandringham apple juice.

The present royal family has, then, adopted seasonal, local and – where possible – organic food for their daily meals and official royal dinners. The aim is to serve wholesome food that tastes of what it is, and tastes the best

196. The Queen's
Diamond Jubilee lunch
in Westminster Hall, 2012.
Most of the tables had
a member of the Royal
Family – including
The Queen – sitting
at them.

197. The Queen and her cousin, the Hon. Margaret Rhodes, enjoy a makeshift lunch on their laps in the sunshine outside the log cabin at Glen Beg on the Balmoral estate.

198. The Duke of Edinburgh fishes for trout on a loch on the Balmoral estate during the royal family's annual summer holiday in September 1971. George V enjoyed fishing the icy pools of the River Dee, and the Queen Mother was an expert fly fisher.

that it can be. It is a million miles from the Cockentrice, as might have been served to Richard II – medieval food that aimed to be what it was not and depended on sauces and spices to enliven it. George III would surely be at home at the modern royal table, as would George V and possibly Elizabeth I, given lots of sweetmeats for dessert. At the end of the meal, Charles II, George IV, Victoria and Edward VII would probably drum their fingers on the table, impatiently waiting for the next course. All would be surprised by the lack of superabundance of meat dishes, and perplexed to find so many vegetables on a royal table. Victoria and Edward VII would be delighted that the banquet was over within two hours, but other monarchs, such as Henry VIII, Charles II and George IV, might expect a four-hour sitting. Most would marvel at the freshness of the food and at the serving hot of so many dishes simultaneously. The lighting, flower displays and organization would also dazzle these visitors from the past. All our monarchs would rejoice to see the buffet of gold and silver-gilt plate still in place, and some might even recognize their own treasures on display. None,

I think, would be able to comment on the taste of individual dishes from the experience of ever having prepared food themselves.

Perhaps we will soon have a cooking king. When he became engaged, Prince William admitted in a television interview to having shared domestic chores while at university, and to having tried his hand at a spot of cooking. The memory elicited a tender smile from his fiancée, so perhaps there is room for improvement. What will be the next course on the menu for the royal family, we will have to wait to find out.

199. Flight Lieutenant Wales shares a meal in the mess with his crew at RAF Valley, Anglesey, 2012.

Further Reading

Maggie Black *et al.*, *A Taste of History: 10,000 Years of Food in Britain*, English Heritage in association with British Museum Press, 1993

Phyllis Pray Bober, *Art, Culture and Cuisine: Ancient and Medieval Gastronomy*, University of Chicago Press, 1999

Peter Brears, *All the King's Cooks: The Tudor Kitchens of King Henry VIII at Hampton Court Palace*, Souvenir Press, 1999

Kate Colquhoun, *Taste: The Story of Britain through its Cooking*, Bloomsbury, 2007

Madeleine Pelner Cosman, *Fabulous Feasts: Medieval Cookery and Ceremony*, George Braziller, 1976

David Duff, ed., *Queen Victoria's Highland Journals*, Hamlyn, 1997

Edwina Ehrman *et al.*, *London Eats Out: 500 Years of Capital Dining*, Philip Wilson, 1999

Susanne Groom *et al.*, *The Taste of the Fire: The Story of the Tudor Kitchens at Hampton Court Palace*, Historic Royal Palaces, 2007

Kathryn Jones, *For the Royal Table: Dining at the Palace*, Royal Collection, 2008

Ian Kelly, *Cooking for Kings: The Life of Antonin Carême, the First Celebrity Chef*, Short Books, 2003

Stephen Mennell, *All Manners of Food: Eating and Taste in England and France from the Middle Ages to the Present*, 2nd edn, University of Illinois Press, 1996

Joycelyne G. Russell, *The Field of Cloth of Gold: Men and Manners in 1520*, Routledge & Kegan Paul, 1969

Pamela A. Sambrook and Peter Brears, eds, *The Country House Kitchen 1650–1900: Skills and Equipment for Food Provisioning*, Sutton Publishing in association with the National Trust, 1996

Roy Strong, *Feast: A History of Grand Eating*, Jonathan Cape, 2002

Gabriel Tschumi, *Royal Chef: Recollections of Life in Royal Households from Queen Victoria to Queen Mary*, William Kimber, 1954

Acknowledgements

I should like to thank Kathryn Jones for answering so many questions on the later chapters of this book, and for her friendly encouragement; Anna Keay for Charles II dining references from her own research; Pam Clark and everyone at the Royal Archives, and Lisa Heighway at the Royal Photographic Archive, Windsor; Brett Dolman for archive information on Nell Gwyn; Deirdre Murphy for guiding me through her collection of rare books on Victoria; Kent Rawlinson for information on the phasing out of Lent; Lee Prosser for a rare early seventeenth-century Danish dining postcard; David Beevers for enjoyable chats on George IV and the Royal Pavilion, Brighton; Marc Meltonville for his help with images, and for much of what I know about practical Tudor and Georgian cooking; Ivan Day for answering the most difficult questions on historic food, and for his help finding images; Rosanna Lewis and Claire Chandler for their meticulous editing; Nicola Bailey for her imaginative design; David Souden for his bright ideas; Clare Murphy for managing the project, for many valuable suggestions and for her warm encouragement and enthusiasm for the project from its inception; and Annie Heron for patiently extracting images from the world's archives.

Picture Credits

Alamy: fig. 153; © From the Collection of Lord Baker of Dorking CH: back cover/jacket, figs. 102, 111; Bayerische Staatsbibliothek, Munich: fig. 26; Bibliothèque nationale de France: figs. 6, 10, 16, 17, 18, 20, 75; The Bodleian Library, University of Oxford: fig. 11 (Douce 374.f.17r); © bpk, Berlin: figs. 21, 46; The Bridgeman Art Library: frontispiece (The Royal Collection © 2013 HM Queen Elizabeth II), figs. 8 (De Agostini Picture Library/M. Seemuller), 38 (Alinari), 53 (Photo © Rafael Valls Gallery, London, UK), 55 (Private collection), 57 (Private collection), 58 (Private collection), 59 (Palazzo Pitti, Florence, Italy), 60 (Fitzwilliam Museum, University of Cambridge, UK), 61 (The Royal Collection © 2013 HM Queen Elizabeth II), 64 (Giraudon), 66 (Private collection), 67 (Private collection), 69 (The Royal Collection © 2013 HM Queen Elizabeth II), 73 (© The Holburne Museum of Art, Bath, UK), 82 (Private collection), 84 (The Stapleton Collection), 110 (The Stapleton Collection), 112 (Yale Center for British Art, Paul Mellon Collection, USA), 113 (© Courtesy of the Warden and Scholars of New College, Oxford), 122 (Private collection), 130 (© Leeds Museums and Art Galleries (Temple Newsam House) UK), 148 (© British Library Board. All Rights Reserved), 150 (Private collection), 155 (Bianchetti/Leemage), 163 (Bianchetti/Leemage), 169 (© Gavin Graham Gallery, London, UK), 176 (Archives Charmet), 180 (Private collection); By permission of the British Library: figs. 1 (C13132-04), 5 (Royal 14E.IV.f.265v), 19 (Harley 4380.f.1r), 40 (Add MS 27699.f.114), 42 (Harley MS 642.f.79v), 87 (069261), 114 (7944.c.4), 120, 125 (7944.c.4), 129 (1406.f.2); © The Trustees of the British Museum: figs. 34, 77 (AN01322141001), 83 (AN207896001), 98 (01335862001-H), 101 (01335865001-H), 108 (AN182884001), 115 (AN01322135001), 118 (11727 2006av7078); © The Devonshire Collection, Chatsworth. Reproduced by permission of the Chatsworth Settlement Trustees: fig. 51; © Ivan Day: fig. 136; By permission of the Trustees of Dulwich Picture Gallery: fig. 139; fotoLibra: figs. 159 (© 2013 Paul W. Hutley), 187 (© 2013 Amoret Tanner Collection); Getty Images: figs. 56, 72 (Paris Match), 151, 167, 168 (Popperfoto), 171 (Gamma-Keystone), 174, 185, 190, 193 (Tim Graham), 198 (Lichfield); The Goldsmiths' Company: fig. 31; Heritage Images: figs. 68 (Stapleton Historical Collection), 88 (The Print-Collector), 160 (Artmedia); Herzog August Bibliothek, Wolfenbüttel: fig. 93 (M:Oe 2.10); Crown copyright: Historic Royal Palaces: figs. 33, 54, 90, 92, 95; © Historic Royal Palaces: figs. 32 (Photo: Robin Forster), 35, 36 (Photo: Nick Guttridge), 37 (Photo: Robert Hoare), 62 (Photo: Paul Barker), 89 (Photo: Claire Collins), 94, 99 (Photo: Robin Forster), 127 (Photo: Claire Collins), 157, 179; © The Hunterian, University of Glasgow 2013: fig. 109; The Imperial War Museum, London: fig. 182; Ian Jones: fig. 192; Kunsthistorisches Museum, Vienna: fig. 27; With assistance of Derek Lawes and the Leyton & Leytonstone Historical Society: fig. 186; City of London, London Metropolitan Archives: figs. 9, 104; Mary Evans Picture Library: figs. 134, 137, 141, 142, 147, 152, 166, 173, 175; Crown Copyright, 2012. Credit: SAC Faye Storer, MOD: fig. 199; Musea Brugge © Lukas-Art in Flanders vzw: fig. 74 (Photo: Hugo Maertens); © Musées de Saint-Omer, B. Jagerschmidt: page 6, fig. 28; Museum Boijmans Van Beuningen, Rotterdam: fig. 12 (Photographer: Studio Buitenhof, The Hague); Courtesy of The Museum of London: figs. 45, 106, 144; The Museum of National History, Frederiksborg: fig. 49; Image courtesy of the National Gallery of Art, Washington: fig. 63 (Samuel H. Kress Collection); © National Portrait Gallery, London: figs. 41, 47, 48, 81 (Private collection, on loan to the National Portrait Gallery, London), 154, 170, 177; © National Trust Images: fig. 172; Prague City Archives (AMP): fig. 65; © Press Association Images: figs. 178 (AP Photo: Oli Scarff), 191 (Photo: Dominic Lipinski), 194 (Photo: John Stillwell); Rex Features: figs. 195, 196 (David Hartley); Taken from *The Final Curtsey* © Margaret Rhodes: figs. 189, 197; © RMN-Grand Palais: figs. 13 (domaine de Chantilly/René-Gabriel Ojéda), 14 (musée du Louvre/Jean-Gilles Berizzi), 25, 100 (musée du Louvre/Hervé Lewandowski); Robert Harding Picture Library/Superstock: fig. 4; Collections Public Library, Rouen. Photograph: Thierry Ascencio-Parvy: figs. 7, 15; The Royal Collection © 2013 HM Majesty Queen Elizabeth II: front cover/jacket, figs. 22, 23, 24, 29, 30, 52, 70, 76, 78, 80, 86, 91, 96, 97, 103 (detail), 105, 116, 117, 119, 124 (detail), 126, 128, 131, 132, 135, 138, 140, 143, 156, 158 (supplied by The Royal Collection – © Reserved), 161, 162, 164, 181, 183, page 208; Royal Museums of Fine Arts of Belgium, Brussels: fig. 50 (Photo: J. Geleyns/Ro scan); The Royal Pavilion and Museums, Brighton & Hove: figs. 121, 123; Rue des Archives: figs. 71, 107; From *Food Mania* by Nigel Garwood and Rainer Voigt. Thames & Hudson Ltd, London: figs. 44, 145, 188; Topfoto.co.uk: figs. 2 (© Roger-Viollet), 43 (The Granger Collection, NYC), 133 (© Fotomas), 184; © Victoria and Albert Museum, London: figs. 39, 79, 146, 149, 165; Wellcome Library, London: fig. 85; Dean and Chapter of Westminster: fig. 3

The publishers have made every effort to trace and contact copyright holders of the illustrations reproduced in this book; they shall be happy to correct in subsequent editions any errors or omissions that are brought to their attention.

Index

For Masha and Malachy

First published 2013 by Merrell Publishers,
London and New York

Merrell Publishers Limited
81 Southwark Street
London SE1 0HX

merrellpublishers.com

in association with

Historic Royal Palaces
Hampton Court Palace
Surrey KT8 9AU

hrp.org.uk

ISBN 978-1-8589-4613-9 (hbk)
ISBN 978-1-8589-4622-1 (pbk)

Produced by Merrell Publishers Limited
Designed by Nicola Bailey
Project-managed by Claire Chandler
Copy-edited by Rosanna Lewis
Indexed by Hilary Bird

Printed and bound in China

AUTHOR BIOGRAPHIES

SUSANNE GROOM was for twenty-four years a curator with Historic Royal Palaces, working on such projects as the restoration of the Tudor kitchens and the Privy Garden at Hampton Court Palace, and on exhibitions at the Banqueting House, Whitehall. Her work centred often on royal life in the eighteenth century at Kew and the palace inhabited there by George III. Her most recent project involved researching the Georgian kitchens at Kew, which opened to the public in 2012.

HESTON BLUMENTHAL is a celebrated chef and the owner of The Fat Duck, a Michelin-starred restaurant in Bray, Berkshire. He has presented several TV shows and is the author of numerous cookery books.

Front jacket/cover: Detail of Robert Taylor Pritchett, *The Golden Jubilee, June–July 1887: The Jubilee State Banquet at Buckingham Palace*, 1887; see fig. 135
Back jacket/cover: James Gillray, *Temperance Enjoying a Frugal Meal*, 1792; see fig. 102
Frontispiece: Detail of Gerrit Houckgeest, *Charles I, Queen Henrietta Maria, and Charles, Prince of Wales, Dining in Public*, 1635; see fig. 69
Page 6: Detail of Cornelius Jacobsz. Delff, *Still Life of Kitchen Utensils*, c. 1600; see fig. 28
Page 208: Detail of James Stephanoff, *The Kitchen, St James's Palace*, published 1819; see fig. 119